INSTANT BLUES HARMONICA
by David Harp

Dedication:

I've dedicated previous versions of this book to the first generation of bluesmen and blueswomen. Their unseen but not unheard presence still inflames my mind, especially when I meditate on the untimely death in 1988 of my friend Mr. J. C. Burris. J. C. learned the blues while serving as seeing-eye kid to his uncle, the late Mr. Sonny Terry. J. C. was perhaps the finest of the solo country blues players, and for me, his death personifies the demise of that entire first generation of Southern Black musicians.

Also to my dear, departed buddy, Tim Janes, who saw the potential of this book way back when it was just a 16 page xerox. Rest in peace, J. C. and Timmy, and wherever you may find yourselves — keep on playing and listening to those blues. And to my more recently demised pal, Mr. Mike Varchol, whose shoes I plan to give tap lessons...

Acknowledgements:

I owe and offer thanks to a multitude of my students, friends, family, mentors, jamming partners, counseling clients, and others too many to mention. But, most importantly, firstly and foremostly, to **Rita** and the **Tadpole** (now known as Katie), for devotion as well as help beyond the call of duty. And last but certainly not least, to **Lily!**

musical i press
Montpelier, Vermont

Seventh Completely Revised Edition
Thirty Fourth Printing

Printed in the State of Vermont by L. Brown and Sons Printing, Inc.

Contents

Read This First

Hi! I'm David Harp. For nearly twenty years, playing blues harmonica has been one of my most entertaining and healthy habits — and I'm really excited about teaching you how to play, too! If you'd like to know a bit more about me, and about how harmonica playing can improve your mind, your body, and even your relationships with other people, please read the section entitled "Why I Wrote This Book". But before you do that, finish reading this section, because it will show you how to use this package in exactly the way that works best for YOU.

Different Strokes for Different Folks

After thirteen years of producing book and cassette instructional methods, I've learned that different people use my packages in different ways. Big Surprise! Some of you prefer to learn by reading, and will read each chapter carefully, before listening to the appropriate section on the tape. Others are listeners, and will mostly just use the cassette, only glancing at the book whenever the tape requests them to.

Some of you will prefer to listen to the entire cassette while flipping through the book, before ever putting "harp" to mouth. Others can't wait, and will start "eating the tin sandwich" after only a bare moment of reading or listening.

Perhaps you'll want to spend one entire lip-weary day mastering all of the material at a single marathon sitting. Or maybe ten or fifteen minutes each day will seem like plenty...

By now, you may already have some ideas about how you are best able to learn new skills. So please feel free to use these materials in a way that will work well for you.

For the convenience of those who prefer not to linger over my every word, I've done three things:

- I've typeset all of the most important words and concepts in **boldface.** Helpful hints, tips and tricks are • bulleted.

- I have **boxed** all of the information that you can't afford to miss, so you can just go from one box to the next.

- I've placed information that some people will desperately need, and others won't need at all, in the four **Appendices** at the back of this book.

Want to be "Jamming" in just a few minutes? If you do, make sure that you've read the entire "Read This First" section, and about the appendices. Then start listening to the cassette, and go directly to the next box, on page 4.

Relax and Enjoy!

For many of us, learning to do something new is a perfect opportunity to dump loads of doubt and self-criticism on ourselves. Just this once, see if you can avoid being hard on yourself. Allow wrong notes to happen without blame — in fact, with blues improvisation, there really are no wrong notes!

If you do find yourself feeling doubtful, insecure, or self-critical, try the "Playing From The Gut" exercise on Page 58. It will help you to just relax and enjoy learning to make music. And just listening to the "play-along" music at the end of the cassette's Side Two will energize and inspire you, when necessary!

When the Going Gets Tough, the Tough Play Harmonica

If you reach a section or an exercise that seems difficult, don't get discouraged and stop. The next section may well be easier, for you. If you do feel tempted to quit, just read the two paragraphs above this one, and try the "Gut" exercise recommended above. It really does help...

The Appendices

Please take a moment right now to read about the four Appendices. Feel free not to use them, unless you want or need to.

Appendix A: The "Musical Idiot" Syndrome

Do you feel at all insecure about your musical abilities? If you've ever considered yourself "unmusical", then you'd better read Appendix A, and take our "Musical I.Q." test. It will help remove any blocks that you may have towards effectively using this method.

Appendix B: An Optional Overview of Music Theory

You don't need to understand music theory in order to play the harmonica. But many people find that their enjoyment of the instrument is increased when they understand why they do what they do. Feel free to either read this section now, or return to it at some other time.

Appendix C: Zen and the Art of Blues Harp Blowing

It may seem funny, that title of Appendix C, but it's no joke. Your mental attitude can really affect your ability to make music. However, I don't want to force any newfangled (or old-fangled) "New Age" type ideas on anybody. So if you believe in the ability of the mind to affect the body, please read Appendix C. It will increase both your enjoyment and the effectiveness of this package. And if you don't believe, ignore Appendix C, and you'll still learn to play the harmonica perfectly well!

Appendix D: More About Your Harmonica

Worried about your *Mississippi Saxophone?* Then turn to page 58.

Why I Wrote This Book

I used to be a self-labeled "musical idiot". I was "tone-deaf", I was "tin-eared", and I "couldn't carry a tune in a bucket". But once I had forced myself to overcome my musical blockage, or musical insecurity, I realized that my former musical idiocy was nothing but a myth. Now I've taught over a hundred thousand people to let music into their lives, and you can learn too!

My own myth of musical idiocy began with a series of negative early experiences with music. As a young child, I enjoyed singing and pretending to play along with records. But a few months of unwanted cello lessons at age 10, and being barred from singing in school when my voice began to change, discouraged me from trying to make music for years, and convinced me of my "tone-deafness". I even took a certain macho pride in being totally unmusical, and liked to joke about it ("I couldn't carry a tune with a handle on it").

However, when my high school friends started a little rock band in 1968, I desperately wanted to be in on the action. Unfortunately, by then everyone believed in my tone-deafness and I was only allowed to carry the equipment on stage and the drunks off.

By 1969, after my first year in college, I decided to emulate my idol, Bob Dylan, by hitch-hiking to Alaska. I grew a scruffy beard (all I could manage at the time) and bought a denim jacket, but something was missing from my costume... what was it? A harmonica!! And then I hit the road, Jack.

I was able to put my unmusical self-image aside at that time for two reasons. Firstly, the late 1960's were a time of great change for me, so I was able to be somewhat flexible as I traded a macho self-image for a more "hippie-type" persona. Secondly, hitch-hiking gave me lots of time among people who didn't already "know" me as unmusical (although some of my first rides quickly noticed my lack of virtuosity, and offered me the choice of shutting up or getting out).

I'm glad now to say that I kept playing that first day, both during my rides and on the side of the road. After 13 or 14 lip-weary hours I picked out my first tune, *"Blowin' in the Wind"*, from a Bob Dylan songbook that I had bought and brought with me. Being able to play even one song gave me confidence, and more good results followed quickly. The more I played, day by day, the more skillful my lips and ears became, and the better I sounded. And the better I sounded, the more I played. By the time I hit Vancouver, I could play a few songs well enough for my fellow travelers to enjoy (the first couple of renditions, anyway). Now, nearly 20 years later, I love to play and teach many kinds of music. **And I'd love to teach you to play the harmonica, today!**

But playing the harmonica isn't *just* fun and creative —it's good for you as well! It can help to exercise your lungs, your lips, and your tongue. It gives you an opportunity to express your emotions and to "blow off steam", musically. It's a wonderful way to meet people (most everybody likes a harmonica player), and a great thing to do with children or other

loved ones. It's good for couples, too. (How could anything that increases the strength and sensitivity of your mouth be bad for your love life?)
And that's enough talk — let's start playing!

I used to be a self-labelled "musical idiot". Now I love to teach, and play, the blues harmonica. Playing harmonica is good for you, and it's easy!

Two Ways to Make Music

There are two very different ways of playing music. Some people prefer one way, some people prefer the other, and many enjoy doing both. I love to play both ways, and hope that you will too.

Classical Music

The word **"classical"** is usually used to describe music composed by European men prior to the 20th century. **But I'd rather use this word to mean *any* piece of music that has been written down, note by note, so that it can be played *exactly* as written.** This definition would include equally pieces by Bach, Beethoven, or the Beatles. Playing classical music will always involve learning to read notes from a notation system like my **HarpTab.**

Improvised Music

"Improvised" music is music created spontaneously by the musician. Although the player may have some preconceived ideas about what he or she is going to play, the notes are neither being read from a sheet of music nor recalled precisely from a memorized tune. Playing improvised music will always involve a certain type of subconscious process that allows the music to "just flow", without thinking about what's going on. I discuss this at length in my "Playing with the Right Side of the Brain" section of Appendix C.

Tape Deck Technique

Practice using your rewind button, so that you can listen to one section of the tape over and over, as many times as you need to.

Important: From now on, scan all title headings (and read any section that interests you). Also look at each picture or chart in between these boxed sections, and glance at all words or sentences in **boldface** type as you go from one box to the next!

About Your Harmonica

There are a number of models and brands of harmonica that are good for playing blues. These "blues-style" harps all have 10 holes, are all tuned to produce a "Major Scale" (I'll explain this on page 26 if you're interested) and range in price between $8.00 and $25.00.

Each harmonica has a little letter, like "G" or "C", stamped on it somewhere. This letter refers to the "letter name" (see page 55) of the lowest note of that particular harmonica. Each "letter" harmonica sounds a bit different. But if you can play one, you can play them all.

I originally began using C harmonicas in my instruction packages. However, I soon noticed that the C harp (which is the most popular for non-blues music) was not the best suited for beginning blues harmonicists, due to the fact that the important "two in" note was difficult to obtain cleanly on a C. I then experimented with many others, discovering that "F" and "G" seemed most appropriate for my teaching purposes.

Unfortunately, I am now unable to obtain enough F or G harmonicas to package with my book and cassette. In fact, for the last few years I've virtually cornered the world market in reasonably priced F and G's! So I've been forced, this year, to switch back to C.

This has affected my teaching method. Since the important hole number "two in" can require a bit of practice (a few minutes, for most beginners), I'll start you off on a blues style that doesn't require its use. This style, called **Third Position Blues**, has been made famous by harmonica greats such as **Little Walter Jacobs, Big Walter Horton, Junior Wells, Norton Buffalo, and Charlie Musselwhite**, to name a few. And *while* you're enjoying Third Position, you'll be practicing that "two in"!

If you didn't get the deluxe edition of this package, complete with professional quality C harmonica, you'll need to buy one.

Please do not try to use any other harp! The tape has been recorded using only C harp, and no other will sound right. So if you try to use that rusty old "G" that's been lying around, it will be more difficult, less satisfying, and you won't be able to play along with my recorded music...

I have four favorite models of harmonica. The Huang brands "Silvertone Deluxe" and "Star Performer" are excellent low-cost (currently about $9) harmonicas for beginner or professional. Hohner's "Golden Melody" (currently about $19) and Tombo's "Lee Oscar" (currently about $22) are also good instruments, though a bit expensive. The aforementioned are all plastic-bodied models, as plastic is preferable to wood for the delicate lips of the would-be harpist (and the sound is just as good). But any 10 hole Major Scale tuned harmonica in C will work just fine.

You will need a ten hole, "standard-tuned" C harmonica to use with this book and cassette. If you don't have one, check out the brands and models recommended above.

If you think that there might be something wrong with your harmonica, please see Appendix D on page 59.

Harmonica Care

• Always rinse your mouth before playing, if you've been eating.

• Don't play it too loudly (for the sake both of harmonica and neighbors).

• Don't keep it in a pocket or purse (unless it's *absolutely* free of lint, change, or other small objects that could get stuck in the holes).

Holding Your Harmonica

At first, almost any way of holding the harmonica is okay. You can think of it as a "tin sandwich", and grab it with either (or both) mitts as you would your tuna fish on whole wheat. I use a one-handed sandwich grip whenever I want to play *while* I do something with my other hand.

However, eventually you'll want to learn to use the effect known as the **"Hand Wah Wah"** (page 34). So, at least sometimes, practice holding your harp in your left hand with fingers flat as pictured. Make sure that the little numbers are visible on top of the harmonica, with the number ten hole to the right.

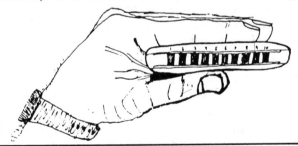

About Your Mouth

When learning to play the harmonica, your mouth will be called upon to do two of the things that it does best. You'll make small movements of the lips and tongue, similar to those that you practice every day while talking. And you'll breathe in and out.

Closing Your Nose

The nose is not normally used in playing the harmonica, although I occasionally play through a nostril to amuse young children, or to discourage inebriated harmonicists at parties from borrowing my instrument. **So practice a moment of breathing through your mouth only, with your nose shut.** If you're not sure how to do that, just think of blowing out the candles on a birthday cake, or drinking a thickshake with a straw. In both cases, you would prevent air from escaping through your nose by tightening certain muscles in the upper back part of your mouth.

Big Mouths and Small

There are three "mouth opening sizes" that you'll learn to use when playing harmonica.

- **The Three Hole Mouth** is easiest. Most mouths just naturally cover about three holes when placed over the harmonica with the teeth almost touching the front of the harp. Try it anywhere on the harmonica, breathing in or out, softly or enthusiastically.

- **The Two Hole Mouth** requires a slight crimping in of the corners of the mouth. You can do this more easily if you pout your lips out slightly, as if you were puckering up for a kiss.

- **The Single Hole Mouth** requires even more crimping and puckering. It's the mouth shape you use when whistling, or drinking through a straw. Your upper lip should be slightly curled up towards your nose, like a dog snarling, rather than curved down to cover your upper front teeth like a camel sneering. **Try to keep your throat and tongue relaxed, even though your lip muscles are tensed.**

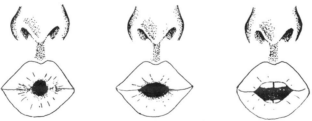

Some people find "single-noting" difficult at first, but fortunately we can play lots of good stuff even before we master it. If you'd like to experiment with single notes, try the number one hole first (both inhaling and exhaling). It's the easiest because there is no number zero hole to worry about! Experiment with the number two hole if you like (breathe through it *very softly*) but don't worry about it, or about single notes at all, for now.

Look at these pictures of mouth sizes, from wide (three hole) to narrow (single hole). *Experiment* with single holing – hole number one is easiest at first.

About Music

If you would like to learn more about music theory and music history, please read Appendix A. The following section will only teach you a few musical terms, and give you a very general and oversimplified idea of why we play what we play.

- Playing any one harmonica hole at a time produces what we call a **note.**

- Playing any two or more holes at the same time produces what we call a **chord.** Chords can be played on any instrument that can play more than one note at a time.

- Harmonica players often like to play along by improvising, or **"jamming"** with a chord or a set of chords played by another instrument, such as a guitar or keyboard.

Scales, the Alphabets of Music

A scale is a specific group of notes, like the "Major Scale" (*Do Re Mi Fa So La Ti Do*) that you may already be familiar with. These specific notes provide the basic building blocks of a piece of music, just like the 26 letters of the alphabet provide the basic building blocks of any piece of writing. The letters of the Russian alphabet create Russian words, sentences, and long somber novels. Letters of the English alphabet create English words, sentences and literature. Scales are different musical alphabets. Three very different scales are most commonly used by harmonica players.

- **The Major Scale has a bouncy, brassy sound.** It is most often used for playing popular, classical, and American folk music.

- **The Minor Scale has a more wistful or plaintive quality.** It is often used in the music of the Gypsy people, in Eastern European music, and in Irish and Jewish folk music.

- **The Blues Scale has, well, a bluesy feel.** Some people consider it a compromise between the Major and Minor Scales, because it uses some notes from both. Developed by the Afro-American people, the Blues Scale is used today in blues, rock, soul, disco, funk and jazz music.

    If you'd like to know more about music, please turn to Appendix B on Page 54. You may at least want to look at the chart on Page 56 which compares these different scales.

Harmonica Positions

Each scale can be played in one or more **positions**. This doesn't refer to playing while standing on your head or lying down, although great music can be created in any posture (and I've tried most of them). The term "position" simply refers to the harmonica note on which a particular scale begins, like C, or D, or G. Just for your information, below is a chart showing the location of each note on your C harmonica. Notice how notes are **repeated** — I'll discuss this on the tape.

Four positions can be used by beginning harmonica players. More will become playable after you learn the advanced technique of note bending, which I'll discuss and demonstrate later.

- The **Major Scale** is most often played in **First Position**. When playing in First Position on a C harmonica, we begin our scale on the note C (there are four of them on your harp). It's easy to play folk, popular, and classical songs in First Position, because it's easy to play a Major Scale starting on C. But it's difficult to play blues in First Position, because it's hard to play a Blues Scale starting on C on a C harp.

- The **Minor Scale** is most often played in **Fifth Position**. When playing in Fifth Position on a C harmonica, we begin our scale on the note A. It's easy to play haunting, beautiful, Minor songs in Fifth Position, like *Greensleeves*, *When Johnny Comes Marchin' Home*, or *Summertime*.

- The **Blues Scale** can be played most easily in either of **two** positions. Playing the Blues Scale in **Third Position** gives us blues music with a Minor, plaintive feel. When playing in Third Position on a C harmonica, we begin our scale on the note D.

- Playing the **Blues Scale** in **Second Position** gives us blues music with a Major, upbeat, bouncy feel. When playing in Second Position on a C harmonica, we begin our scale on the note G. Second Position is sometimes called "Cross Position" or "Cross Harp".

The term **"position"** simply refers to the harmonica note on which a particular scale begins. We'll begin playing in First Position, then go to Third, then Second. Remember those names if you can, but don't worry about them.

Hole Number:	1	2	3	4	5	6	7	8	9	10
This note plays when you breathe: **In**	D	G	B	D	F	A	B	D	F	A
This note plays when you breathe: **Out**	C	E	G	C	E	G	C	E	G	C

Developing Rhythm

If you've ever tapped your foot while listening to your favorite band, you already understand how a **beat** is the pulse that underlies a piece of music. **Rhythm** might be defined as the way in which we break that beat into even smaller parts.

Blues music is often divided into four beat units called "measures" or **"bars"**. So practice tapping your foot while you say *"**one** two three four **one** two three four"*. Emphasize each "one" by saying it louder, and try to make sure that each foot tap takes the exact same amount of time as the rest. Use one foot tap for each count, (one tap, two tap, etc.) If this seems hard, try doing it *while* you walk.

Each beat is composed of two parts. The **downbeat** occurs exactly as your foot hits the floor. The **upbeat** is the time that passes between downbeats.

My notation system, called HarpTab™, uses a dot • to show you where the downbeat falls. Try saying this, just as I do on the cassette:

•   •   •   •   •   •   •   •

Dir-ty   Dir-ty   Dog   Dir-ty   Dir-ty   Dog

Notice how the "Dir" happens just as my foot hits the floor, and the "ty" happens while my foot is rising up between taps. There is also one tap that could be called a **"beat of silence"**, after each "Dog". Each three word phrase with its beat of silence forms one single four beat bar. Beats of silence are convenient times to breathe — take advantage of them, and take a breath!

Blues musicians often like to emphasize the downbeats. This is called **swinging** the beat. Now say some swingin' Dirty Dogs by saying the "dir" parts louder and holding them for a touch longer, as I do.

You'll understood rhythm much better by *hearing* about it than by *reading* about it. So listen to the recorded section on rhythm, a few times if necessary. And if you can say a few "swingin' Dirty Dogs", you've got rhythm!

Each Dot • represents one tap of your foot.

From now on, say or play each exercise that you see notated (like the Dirty Dirty Dogs). If an exercise seems hard to understand, read the next box below it. If that doesn't help enough, you'll just have to break down and read the entire section, or listen to the tape a few more times.

The Art of Articulation

Focus your attention onto your tongue and the roof of your mouth, and say the syllable "Da". Do it again, more forcefully. You'll probably notice that you begin with your nose shut, and the tip of your tongue pushed up against the roof of your mouth. Air pressure builds up behind your tongue. Then suddenly your tongue drops, and the "Da" rushes out like a dam bursting.

Now try saying "Ta". Feels almost the same as "Da", right? But "Ka" feels different, because you're raising the back of the tongue to block the air flow, instead of the tip. Say "Tuka", and observe the use of both the tip and the back of your tongue. **Whisper** these nonsense syllables a few more times, and notice that the tongue movements are exactly the same, whether you are whispering them or saying them out loud.

Using the tongue to break up the flow of air through the mouth is called **articulation**. It's one of the most important techniques used to create rhythms, so spend a moment now practicing the following articulation rhythms.

"Dirty Dirty Dog" should be familiar by now. Feel free to substitute other syllables if you prefer (or if you feel funny saying the Dirty Dogs out loud). "Dada Dada Da" works just as well, if you keep the same rhythm as demonstrated on the tape. Don't leave out the beat of silence in each of the two following four beat (one bar) rhythms!

•   •   •   •   •   •   •   •

Dirty   Dirty   Dog   Dada   Dada   Da

Here's an eight beat (or two bar) rhythm pattern, with three beats of silence. Once again, use "Da" and "Dada" or "Ta" and "Tata" instead of Dirty and Dog, if you like. I'll be using these syllables interchangeably from now on.

•   •   •   •   •   • • •

Dirty   Dirty   Ding   Dong   Dog

•   •   •   •   •   • • •

Dada   Dada   Da   Da   Da

Create a 16 beat (four bar) rhythm pattern by combining two of the four beat patterns with one eight beat pattern, like this:

•   •   •   •   •   •   •   •

Dirty   Dirty   Dog   Dada   Dada   Da

•   •   •   •   •   • • •

Dirty   Dirty   Ding   Dong   Dog

—11—

Say the preceding four bar pattern a few times, and then say it along with me. Of course it feels a bit funny! I'll play a few seconds of rhythm track, so that you can feel the beat. Then I'll say "one two three GO!", and we'll start articulating along with the background music. We'll also do a 16 beat variation on the one we just did:

•	•	•	•	•	•	•	•
Dog	Dog	Dirty	*Dirty*	Dog	Dog	Dirty	*Dirty*

•	•	•	•	•	•		
Dog	Dog	Dirty	Dog	Dog	*dirty dirty dirty*		

and then another 16 beater, made of of two four beaters (including one bar that has a beat of silence in its *middle*) plus an eight beater:

•	•	•	•	•	•	•	•
Dirty	Dog	Dog		Dirty		Dog	

•	•	•	•	•	• • •
Dirty	Dirty	Dirty		Dog	

Now you can do either of two things. Take the four and eight beat rhythm patterns that I've given you, and put them together in various combinations. Or else make up some four, eight, or sixteen beat rhythm patterns of your own.

Wooziness?

Some people feel light-headed when they first begin to play, due to excess oxygen passing through the lungs. If this happens, you can either stop playing for a moment, play more softly (which uses less air), or sit down and keep playing.

Eventually you'll get used to the increased air flow, and the wooziness will only occur if you play very enthusiastically. I like to run while playing (it's not hard, if you can already run without playing), and occasionally feel a bit high when I really push myself. It's fun, but I can't recommend it because I suppose that it would be possible to pass out and fall while doing it.

Listen to the tape, then use your tongue to break up your breath by saying "Da" sounds like the ones above. Doing this is called **articulation**.

Blues rhythm patterns are usually four, eight, or sixteen beats long, and are divided into four beat units called **bars**.

HarpTab™

HarpTab™, short for Harmonica Tablature Notation System, is my simple way of writing down harmonica music. It tells you which hole or holes to breathe in or out on, and for how long. It works like this:

- **Numbers refer to the hole numbers 1 through 10** on top of your harmonica.

- I means **breathe In**.

- O means **breathe Out**.

- **Dots** • represent **downbeats**, and tell you **how long to hold a note**.

For example: 4   means breathe out on the hole marked 4.
              O

And 6 means breathe in on the hole marked 6.
    I

If **two or more holes are supposed to be played together** (as a chord) they will be **underlined**.

For Example: 4 5   means breathe out on holes number 4 and 5.
               O

If I need to describe a note while writing a line like this, I'll put an In or Out **next to** the numerical hole number, not under it. So **4 5 Out** would mean breathe out on holes number four and five, and **5 In** would mean breathe in on hole number five.

Where the Heck Is Hole Number Seven (or Eight, or Three)?

None of the music that you're going to play now requires the use of single notes. For that reason, it isn't too important, yet, to be able to find any specific hole. Later on, it will be. For now, just kind of generally **aim** at the holes you want, high end, low end, or middle.

If you need a bit more help with this, here are a few tips on locating whichever hole you want to play. They might help you do the next exercise. Soon, you won't need tricks like these, because the more you play, the easier it gets to find your way around on the old "ten holer".

For some, the temptation is to try to locate a particular hole by keeping your eyes on the little numbers on the cover plate. This will rapidly make you cross-eyed, however, since as the harp approaches your mouth you can no longer see the numbers. So let's forget about that method right now!

Fortunately, the mouth is one of the most sensitive and quick-learning organs of the body. This is due to the fact that a large portion of the brain is devoted to operating the mouth (although hearing certain people talk may make you wonder about that). So your lips will quickly learn exactly where every hole is, after a few hours of playing.

At first, however, you may need to "count holes" from the left with your tongue-tip to make sure that you are on the desired one. Or you can find a particular hole by holding your harp between the tips of your thumb and forefinger, with your forefinger tip precisely centered over the hole you want. Then just touch your forefinger to the center of your upper lip and presto! There you are!

If you have trouble finding the notes to use in the following exercise, check out the two little tricks above. They'll help.

Bouncy Blowin': A First Position Jamm

Ready for your first Jamm Session? I hope so, because it's time to go for it! You've already learned everything you need to know to play along with some simple keyboard music. We'll be playing along with a C chord, which means that we're in First Position. Our jamm will sound more happy and bouncy than bluesy, but that's okay for now. We'll get down home and funky in our *next* jamm session!

A Quick Review

- Put your mouth over holes four and five, just slightly to the left of the middle of your harmonica.

- Your upper and lower front teeth should be no more than a quarter inch apart. They should be almost, but not quite touching the front of the harp.

- Put the harmonica well in between your lips.

- Start out with a good lungful of air, and keep your **nose shut**.

- Blow out, using your tongue to **whisper** (don't say it out loud) a Dirty Dirty Dog type pattern. **Remember, O means breathe Out!**

•	•	•	•	•	•	•	•
Dirty	Dirty	Dog		Dada	Dada	Da	
<u>45</u>	<u>45</u>	<u>45</u>		<u>45</u>	<u>45</u>	<u>45</u>	
Out	Out	Out		O	O	O	

Whisper the above *through* your harp. Catch a quick inhaled breath during the beat of silence, by opening your mouth while keeping the harmonica firmly pressed into position against your upper lip. This lets you breathe *silently* around the harmonica instead of noisily through it.

Now do the same thing along with my keyboard backing, just as I do on the tape. Stay on the 4 and 5 Out, and articulate some of the other rhythm patterns from page 12.

Movin' It Around

All of the Out notes (which happen to be, on a C harmonica, notes of a C chord) will sound just fine when played along with the C keyboard play-along backing. You can play any Out notes, in any combination — you just can't go wrong! Following are a few ideas and techniques that will help you to create your own improvisations, as well as a few **licks** that I like to use.

Licks and Riffs

Licks (also called **riffs**) are note combinations that you memorize, so that you can use them in appropriate places without having to think much. They're a bit like cliches, or favorite expressions which are part of your verbal bag of tricks. You can create licks of your own (we'll learn lots more about that, later), or memorize mine, or both. As you get to know your instrument better, you will be able to learn licks from records and tapes.

I'll only be writing down the most famous or important licks, and not every riff that I play on the tape. I'd like you to use my taped demonstations for inspiration or to provide examples. But I'd prefer if you *didn't* attempt to copy my licks exactly. Although the rhythms are important to learn, the actual notes that you use with the patterns are *yours* to create. I'll provide the guidelines, and give examples. You'll come up with your own versions.

Your First Lick

Let's start by moving the harmonica just a little bit, for the Up and Down Dirty Dirty Dog Lick, as it is popularly known.

Begin on holes number four and five. **Make sure that your lips are wet, so that the harmonica *slides* rather than pulls.** Move up to holes five and six for the first "Dog", then down to holes number three and four for the second, as notated below:

•	•	•	•		•	•	•	•
Dirty	Dirty	Dog			Dada	Dada	Da	
<u>45</u>	<u>45</u>	<u>56</u>			<u>45</u>	<u>45</u>	<u>34</u>	
Out	Out	Out			O	O	O	

Learning the Distance Between Holes

At first, it's hard to tell how far to move the harmonica to go from one hole to the next. It's easy to accidentally stay on the original hole (that is, not move far enough) or to end up two holes away (move too much).

The actual distance between holes is about 5/16 of an inch, for all the good that knowing it will do you. It's just a matter of practice. Listen to my demonstrations, and spend just one or two minutes a day practicing the taped distance exercise. You'll get it *eventually*, and you don't *really* need it now!

More First Position Licks

Try a 16 beat Up and Down Dog lick like this one:

•	•	•	•		•	•	•	•
Dirty	Dirty	Dog			Dada	Dada	Da	
<u>45</u>	<u>45</u>	<u>56</u>			<u>45</u>	<u>45</u>	<u>34</u>	
Out	Out	Out			O	O	O	

•	•	•	•	•	• • •
Dirty	Dirty	Ding	Dong	Dog	
<u>45</u>	<u>45</u>	<u>56</u>	<u>56</u>	<u>45</u>	
Out	Out	Out	O	O	

And here's another 16 beater, the Low to High Dog lick. Don't worry much about being on exactly the notes I've written, as I've just notated this one to give you some reading practice. Just generally go from low to high. Make absolutely sure that your lips are wet for this one!

•	•	•	•		•	•	•	•
Dirty	Dirty	Dog			Dada	Dada	Da	
<u>12</u>	<u>23</u>	<u>34</u>			<u>34</u>	<u>45</u>	<u>56</u>	
Out	Out	Out			O	O	O	

•	•	•	•	•	• • • •
Dirty	Dirty	Ding	Dong	Dog	
56	67	78	89	9 10	
Out	O	O	O	O	

Get the idea? Try the High to Low Dog lick now, by starting around holes nine and ten and working your way down to the low end. And try the Low to Middle back then to Low Dog lick as well. Just listen to me do them and describe them on tape! It's easy!

Make up some licks yourself, using the other rhythm patterns from page 12 with a variety of high, middle and low Out notes. Or make up some rhythms of your own, and blow 'em out anywhere through your harmonica!

The Slide

With your lips well wetted, slide from one end to the other, from high to low, and from low to high, as demonstrated. Try the Dirty Dog Slide lick: start low, slide up to the middle on the "Dir" syllable, and back down on the "ty". Slide up and down again for the second Dirty, then just slide low to middle for the final Dog. Do the same motions again, but going from middle to high.

When sliding, you can either hold your head still, and move your harmonica, or hold your harmonica steady and move your head. Works perfectly well either way.

The Jump

Instead of sliding smoothly, we can also cover long distances on the harmonica by **jumping** from place to place. Try jumping back and forth from the one hole to the ten, then back, or any other distances.

Wet your lips and sliiiide around in the Dirty Dog (or any other) rhythm, just as I do on the cassette. Turn the lights down low and the tape up high, listen to my examples of licks, slides, and jumps, then jamm some yourself!

Use some of the hints, tricks, and licks above, or make up your own. As long as you stick to the OUT notes, you literally can't go wrong!

If you feel inhibited or nervous about jamming, it might be worth your while to spend a few moments now with the exercises in Appendix C (Page 57).

A Few More Rhythm Patterns

Here are a few more useful eight beat rhythm patterns to try. The first one demonstrates **anticipation** — its second four beat phrase begins on the upbeat "Da" just before the first downbeat of the bar. The last two patterns will prove very useful later on, so at least say them a few times to yourself (or out loud, why be shy?). They're long, so start empty or you'll get too full before you finish.

Dirty   Dirty   Dog   Da Dirty   Dirty   Dog

Dirty   Dirty   Dirty   Dirty   Dirty   Dirty   Dog

Dirty   Dirty   Dirty   Dirty   Dirty   Dog   Dog

About Saliva

Like it or not, saliva is a fact of life. And it usually seems as though there are only two salivary conditions: too much, and too little.

You have too little saliva if it is hard to keep your lips wet when sliding. If this is a problem, keep a glass of water handy.

Excess saliva tends to get caught in the reeds of your harmonica to cause what I call **saliva blocks**. A saliva block temporarily causes the reed to get stuck, so that it doesn't seem to want to play. Fortunately, inhaling or exhaling with vigor will always remove a saliva block.

If saliva blockage becomes a problem for you, try to play with your head tilted slightly up, so that any excess saliva tends to stay in your mouth. I know that it sounds yucky, but after all, it was there in the first place, wasn't it?

In Articulation

It's easy to do harmonica articulation on the exhale — as easy as talking, which most of us practice for hours each day. It's not quite as easy to articulate on the In breath. In fact, it may take as much as a few moments of practice to get the hang of it! So give it a try, but please don't feel discouraged or be hard on yourself if it doesn't come naturally or instantly. It's not a natural thing to do. So begin working on In articulations, but don't get hung up here.

Remember thinking about the "Da" and "Ka" tongue motions involved in articulation? Say a few "Da"s right now, focusing your attention on your tongue. Empty your lungs, shut your nose, and see if you can say a few "Da"s on the inhale. Begin with your tongue pushed up against the roof of your mouth, and try to inhale (but your tongue is blocking all air from entering). Suddenly, let your tongue fall, and a "Da" will shoot in! For In articulations, **"Doo"s or "Too"s** may feel more natural than "Da"s.

See if you can whisper a few **inhaled** "Da"s or "Doo"s, without your harp. Remember, start with lungs **empty,** mouth close to single hole width, or at least not too wide, and nose **shut.** As it starts to feel a bit more natural after a moment of practice, try that familiar old "Dirty Dirty Dog", or "Doo Doo DooDoo Doo".

Practice some In articulations through the <u>45</u> chord. If "Dirty Dirty Dog" is hard to inhale, try "Doodoo Doodoo Doo", or "Tootoo Tootoo Too". You may find that when articulating on an In note, it's easier if your lips are as close to a single note opening as you can manage (or at least no more than two holes wide).

In First Position, all of the Out notes can be used for easy and error free improvisation (the Simple First Position Jamm Rule). In **Third Position, all of the In notes from 4 to 10 can be used (the Simple Third Position Jamm Rule).**

Tense Notes, Relaxed Notes

Obviously, more notes than just the ones described above can be used in First and Third Positions. The two simple rules (First = all Out notes, Third = 4 through 10 In) *work*, but they exclude many perfectly good notes, as just a moment's look at the note chart of page 9 will show. For instance, if the 3, 6, and 9 Out notes (all G notes) work in First Position, why not the 2 In? That's a G note also...

The answer, of course, is that these rules are provided to help you start playing. They keep you on the "safe" notes. Safe notes?

When people listen to music (whether played by themselves or by someone else), they have a set of **musical expectations**. For instance, if we hear the beginning notes of *Happy Birthday*, we would not expect to suddenly hear some notes taken from *The Star Spangled Banner*. Even when we are improvising, like we've just been doing with my play-along music, we have certain expectations.

When improvising, we expect that the notes played will *more or less* match the background music. I say more or less, because when we improvise we *want* our expectations to be broken at least part of the time. If our expectations are never broken, then we consider the improvisation to be boring. Notes that fulfill our expectations I call **"safe" notes,** or relaxed notes. They feel comfortable, restful. Notes that break our expectation I call **"tense" notes.**

The Out notes that you used in the First Position jamm are *all* very safe. That's why the Simple First Position Rule jamm gets kind of old after a few hours — there's just not enough tension in it, and our expectations are *never* broken.

The Simple Third Position Jamm Rule includes both safe and tense notes. You can demonstrate this for yourself, as I do on the tape. Just play 45 In along with my Third Position backing in D minor, then move up to 67 In, then back to 45 In. The 45 In chord will feel the *rightest*.

As I gradually increase the number of notes that you can use when playing, I'll give you some increasingly tense notes, and it will become easier to feel which notes are more relaxed and which are more tense.

All of the musical hints and rules that I give you are like training wheels on a bicycle. They make your playing easy and safe at first, but if you use them for *too* long, they hold you back.

Also: As I said before, try to play *all* pieces that I've written out for you, or at least look at the notation *while* you listen to my demonstration on the cassette.

Now it's time to play some Third Position licks, using the notes 4 through 10 In. You may notice that you need to use **less air** on the higher notes. Be gentle — you don't always need to play loudly!

Try our old Dirty Dirty Dog standby, using all In notes:

•	•	•	•		•	•	•	•
Dirty	Dirty	Dog			Dada	Dada	Da	
45	45	56			45	45	34	
I	I	I			I	I	I	

•	•	•	•	•	• • •
Dirty	Dirty	Ding	Dong	Dog	
45	45	56	56	45	
I	I	I	I	I	

Also try a 16 beat Low to High Dirty Dog lick using In notes (just as you did using Out notes on page 16), and a 16 beat High to Low Dog lick. See if you can apply some of the rhythm patterns on pages 12 and 18 to your 4 through 10 In notes. I'll demonstrate some variations on tape, and leave some room for you to make up your own.

Shakin' and Slidin' (Shake In and Slide In)

Sliding works just as well on the In notes as it does on the outs, so wet your lips, and glide! Use the same slide timings as you did on the Out breaths (page 17), or make up new ones. I often like to pull the harp away from my lips at the end of a slide; it makes for a nice trailing off effect.

You'll get a clearer sound out of your In slides if you use as close to a single hole mouth position as you can manage. With single holing, you can also use the exciting **shake** technique.

Place your single hole size mouth over the 4 hole. Breathe in, then move to 5 In, then back to 4 In. When you can do it quickly, you can get a wonderful warble sound. It's worth beginning to practice learning the distance between holes (page 16) for this technique alone! And once you learn it, you can shake while playing any lick for an extra kick! Here's a good eight bar shake lick. **Notice my shake underline notation:**

••••   • • • •   •   •   •   •   • • • •

<u>45</u>   <u>56</u>   (repeat twice more)   <u>89</u>   <u>78</u>   <u>67</u>   <u>56</u>   <u>45</u>
www   www   www www www www
I   I   I   I   I   I   I

Spend a few minutes adding shakes and slides to your other Third Position licks and rhythm patterns. Play along with the backing music, and feel free to play solo (by yourself) as well.

Little Walter Third Position Lick

Marion Walter Jacobs (1930 - 1968) is considered by many blues lovers to have been the greatest harmonicist ever. He played both chromatic harmonica (see pages 60-62 if you're curious about "chro") and ten hole using Third Position.

The following lick is similar to a theme used by Walter during the last five verses of ***Thunderbird*** (the first three verses of the song are played in Second Position using a G harmonica). Although Walter used a chromatic in these verses, you can play along using your C ten hole in Third Position. Other good Walter songs that you can play along with on C harp are: ***Teenage Beat*** (all Third Position), ***Flying Saucer*** (begins in Third, goes to Second using a G), and ***Blue Lights*** (begins in Third, goes to Second using a G, ends in Third). All are found on the excellent Chess Blues Masters Series *Little Walter* double album (2ACMB-202).

Notice that the change from <u>45</u> In to <u>34</u> In is anticipated, and occurs slightly before the beat (and so the <u>34</u> In note lasts longer than any of the others). I indicate that by positioning the <u>34</u> to the **left** of the dot. To make the lick more like the original, we must also anticipate the first beat by sliding up to the first <u>45</u> In. It also sounds better if we slide rather than jump between the <u>34</u> In and the <u>56</u> In.

•   •   •   •   •   • • •

Da Dog   Dog   Dirtyyyyyyyy   Dog

•   •   •   •   •   • • •

\ <u>45</u>   <u>45</u>   <u>45</u>   <u>34</u>   <u>56</u>
   In   In   I   I   I

Try playing the Walter lick three times, for a total of six bars (24 beats). Finish off a bluesy sounding eight bar pattern by applying the same rhythm pattern while you move from the high end to the middle, ending on 45 In. This two bar ending might look something like this:

•	•	•	•	•	• • •
45	45	45	34	56	(repeat twice more)
In	In	I	I	I	

•	•	•	•	•	• • •
89	78	67	56	45	
I	I	I	I	I	

Here's something to look forward to: as your technical skill increases, you'll get increasingly interesting licks from master harpists to work on!

Chord Structures

Sometimes blues musicians play along with a single chord for extended periods of time. Playing like that is often called playing a "boogie". Up until now, we've been using only one chord at a time to play along with.

Most often musicians like to play along with a repeated pattern, or structure, composed of two or more chords. Chord structures are also sometimes called **chord changes**.

Here's a simple four bar long, two chord structure. It's called a two chord structure because it begins to repeat itself after just two chords. It's called a four bar structure because each repeated **verse** is four bars long. It allows you to use the two positions, First and Third, that you've already practiced.

Play any Third Position (4 through 10 In) licks during the D Minor chord for eight beats. Play any First Position (1 through 10 Out) licks during the C Major chord for eight beats. Use articulations, slides, and shakes as you like.

•••• ••••	•••• ••••		•••• ••••	•••• ••••
D Minor	C Major	repeat	D Minor	C Major
4 - 10 In	1 - 10 Out		4 - 10 In	1 - 10 Out

Sometimes it's fun to try to play approximately the same lick for each chord. We can do this by changing the notes from Ins to Outs or from Outs to Ins, but keeping the rhythm pattern and the way we move the harmonica through our mouths (low to high, or high to low, or four beats of 45 then one beat of 56 then three beats of silence, for example) the same.

This style of playing is called **thematic playing**, because in it we take one musical theme or lick and make slight changes in it. Of course, we'll want to break some expectations by varying the theme somewhat, perhaps by changing the rhythm pattern a bit or by throwing in a slightly altered set of notes. Listen to me vary the Dirty Dirty Ding Dong Dog eight beat theme on cassette (notice how I take some liberties with the three beats of silence), and try some variations of your own.

The Ins and Outs of Jamming

You've practiced the Outs. You've practiced the Ins. Now it's time to gain full conscious control over what has been both natural and necessary since birth — your breathing!

Using both the In and Out notes *together* makes for much more interesting music than can be obtained by either alone. That's because the Out notes include some notes that are very tense when used in Third Position. Some of the In notes can be used to create tension in First Position, but it's difficult to use them effectively until you can bend notes (more on that, later).

Our old standby, the Dirty Dirty Dog rhythm pattern, works well with combined In and Out notes. Practice this rhythm breathing pattern for a moment, without your harp. Remember: nose closed!

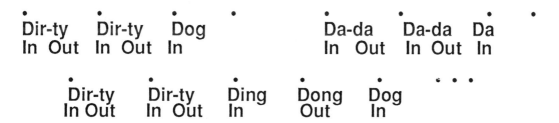

| Dir-ty | Dir-ty | Dog | | Da-da | Da-da | Da |
| In | Out | In | | In | Out | In |

| Dir-ty | Dir-ty | Ding | Dong | Dog |
| In | Out | In | Out | In |

Practice this breathing pattern on the 45 In and 45 Out for a moment, then take it on the road — move it around! Start around four, and use the first eight beats to inhale and exhale your way up to the high end. Take the last eight beats to work your way back down to the 45 In again. If you like, use one of the Ins to **slide** on (the first or last In work best as slides).

This eight beat rhythm pattern also works well as an In/Out breathing rhythm.

•		•		•		•			•		•		•

Dir-ty   Dir-ty   Dir-ty Dir-ty   Dir-ty   Dir-ty Dog
In Out In Out   In Out In Out   In Out   In Out In

Practice it on <u>45</u>, then move it around in any way that you like between 4 and 10. I like to start on <u>9 10</u>, wend my way down to <u>45</u>, then head on up to <u>67</u> or <u>78</u>. What sounds good to you? If you invent a lick that you especially like, try writing it down in HarpTab so you don't forget it.

A John Mayall Style Lick

This breathing rhythm will produce a lick similar to that used by John Mayall in his famous 1970 song, ***Room To Move.*** It's also similar to a Sonny Boy Williamson II lick used in a song called ***One Way Out.***

Try it first without harp, and then on <u>45</u>. Remember: Nose shut! Notice the fast one beat Out/In on the sixth beat, with the **emphasis (In!)** on the In note. It is this rhythmic change that breaks our expectations in this exciting and popular lick!

•		•		•		•			•		•		•

In In   Out   In In   Out   In In   Out In!

An Easy Way to Do An Advanced Lick

This is strange, but it works and sounds just great! Take a two inch long piece of 1/2 inch wide Scotch® tape, and carefully cover holes number 2 and 3 with the tape. Make sure that you cover both holes completely. The 1/2 inch wide tape will just barely cover both holes, if you position it precisely. If you fold about 1/4 inch of each end of the tape over, so that it sticks to itself, it will be easier to remove the tape later.

Now cover holes 1 through 4 with your mouth. You'll have to open wider than usual to do this. It's okay if your upper and lower teeth want to rest on the upper and lower cover plates of the harmonica. Breathe *gently* in and out, so that you get a rich, organ-like sound from your <u>14</u> chord.

As I play a D minor/C Major chord structure (four beats of each chord), play a four beat articulation on the In breath, then a four beat articulation pattern on the Out breath. Use Dirty Dirty Dogs, or any other pattern that you like. Simple, isn't it? But strangely satisfying...

About Tongue Blocking and Single Notes

By the way, this technique is known as the **octave block**, since the 1 and 4 holes provide octave notes (see Appendix B, page 54), for more on octaves). Usually the *tongue* is used to block the middle two holes, but that's not as easy as using tape. Experiment with tongue blocking if you like, but don't get frustrated — it's Volume Two stuff!

Many non-blues harmonica players use a modification of the octave block tongue position to obtain single holes. They cover four holes with their mouth, then block either the three leftmost holes or the three rightmost holes with the tip and side of their tongue. It's hard to do, and not too useful for blues music. Blues harpists almost always prefer to get single holes by puckering up as though they were whistling, so that their mouths cover only one hole.

Using the Mayall Style Rhythm

Try a Mayall style breathing pattern that you just learned on the 14. Sounds great, doesn't it? Or combine some 14 In/Out licks with some 4 through 10 In only licks, two bars each.

• • • •   • • • •   • • • •   • • • •

14 In/Out licks   4 through 10 In licks

This style of playing will sound good with my D minor backing, or played without any backing at all. Playing without any background music is called playing **solo**.

You can also do something similar by combining the 14 In/Out licks with the moving around In/Out licks between 4 and 10. When playing by yourself, you can do eight beats of each, as notated below, or four beats of each, or sixteen, as you prefer.

• • • •   • • • •   • • • •   • • • •

14 In/Out licks   4 through 10 In/Out licks

One Last Blues-Rock Rhythm

Following is one of my favorite blues-rock rhythms, similar to that used in the song *Tequila.* It's not easy, so listen to it many times before even trying to *say* it. Once you can say it, see if you can *breathe* it. And once you can breathe it, play it through the 45 or 14 chords.

•   •   •   •   •   •   •   •

Dirty   Dirty   Diggety   Dirty   Dirty   Dirty   Dog

•   •   •   •   •   •   •   •

In In   Out Out   In In In   Out Out   In In   Out Out   In

This *Tequila* breathing rhythm can also be moved around. Try it from high to middle, or from middle to high. You can either stay on the same note or notes for *two* beats (so that you use the same notes for In In Out Out), or you can move from note to note with *every* beat. Listen to my examples, then experiment.

Be daring! Turn the last In into a slide, or use the <u>14</u> chord for the first four beats of the pattern, then jump to the high end and work your way down for the last three beats!

Playing "Classical" Music

As I discussed earlier, in the section entitled "Two Ways of Making Music", I often use the word "classical" to mean any piece of music which has been written down so that it can be played over and over again in exactly the same way. Of course, the word also can be used to refer to music created and written down by European men in the seventeenth, eighteenth, and nineteenth centuries.

In this chapter, I'll provide you with a few folk songs, popular songs, classical songs, and hints on figuring out hits from the sixties. If these don't hold much interest for you, please skim the section headings and read all boxes on your way to page 35, "Where The Blues Began". But try one song, at least...

The Major Scale

As I said in my Scales section (page 8, with more in Appendix B), scales are musical alphabets. The alphabet on which most popular, folk, and classical songs are based is called the Major Scale. It is most easily played between holes 4 and 7.

Since you may not be able to get single notes yet, don't worry about them. Although I will notate the Major Scale as though you were playing single notes, you can just try to "aim" or "center" your mouth on the hole that's written down, and let the holes on either side of it creep in. It *is* getting towards time to work on single notes, though, so spend a few minutes with that section, below, as soon as you feel like it.

Play the Major Scale both from left to right and from right to left. Notice that the Out/In pattern on the first three holes changes for the fourth:

Do	Re	Mi	Fa	So	La	Ti	Do
4	4	5	5	6	6	7	7
Out	In	Out	In	Out	In	In	Out

Mr. Hohner and The Case of the Missing Notes

A case could be made that the *Sheng,* a Chinese instrument made up of multiple pipes and reeds, is the forefather of the harmonica. But everybody agrees that the first *modern* harmonica was made by Mr. Matthias Hohner of Germany, in the 1830's.

Mr. Hohner's instrument was created for the purpose of playing German folk and classical music, most of which was based on the Major Scale. So he arranged the little metal vibrating reeds inside the holes in such a way that it was easy to play a Major Scale. He also managed to arrange the notes so that covering any number of the Out notes and blowing would always produce either the first, the third, or the fifth note of the Major Scale. These particular notes are the ones that form the chord known as the C Major Chord.

In order to make neighboring notes sound OK when played together, Mr. Hohner was omitted notes from the harmonica in two places, and double up on a note in one place. This is why we can only *easily* play a complete Major Scale CDEFGABC between holes 4 and 7. As you can see, there are missing Major Scale notes in holes 2, 3, and 10. These missing notes can be supplied by the mysterious process of bending, as you will no doubt eventually demonstrate for yourself.

Hole Number:	1	2	3	4	5	6	7	8	9	10
This note plays when you breathe: **In**	D	G	B	D	F	A	B	D	F	A
This note plays when you breathe: **Out**	C	E	G	C	E	G	C	E	G	C

Major Scale Songs

The following songs are based on the Major Scale. Choose the one that you know best, and try to play it while looking at the notation. Some of you will prefer to play just a few notes at a time, learning the song section by section. Others will want to plow through an entire song, mistakes and all.

You can use the "aim" or "center" method of locating your mouth over the hole that I've written down, or you can begin to work on getting single notes, as discussed in the section following these songs.

So pick your favorite, and take your time. There are really only two things to think about: which hole to use (you have ten choices), and whether to inhale or exhale (two choices). So take a few deep breaths or use the relaxation and visualization exercise in Appendix C if you feel nervous. It's like jumping into a cool pool of water: hard to get started, but fun once you do it!

- **"Oh When The Saints Go Marching In"**: Try some hand wah-wahs (page 34) on the longer held notes – play it fast for a party, slow for a New Orleans funeral.

•	•	•	•••••	•	•	•	•••••
Oh	when	the	saints	go	mar-	chin	in
4	5	5	6	4	5	5	6
O	O	I	O	O	O	I	O

•	•	•	••	••	••	••	••••••
Oh	when	the	saints	go	mar-	chin	in
4	5	5	6	5	4	5	4
O	O	I	O	O	O	O	I

•	•	•••	•	••	•	•	•	•••••
Yes	I	want	to	be	in	that	num-	ber
5	4	4	4	5	6	6	6	5
O	I	O	O	O	O	O	O	I

•	•	••	••	••	••	•••••
When	the	saints	go	mar-	chin	in
5	5	6	5	4	4	4
O	I	O	O	O	I	O

- **"Michael Row The Boat Ashore"**: Notice that some notes fall on the upbeats, so watch your foot as you play (and keep that foot-beat steady).

•	•	••		•	•	••	•	•	••••	••
Mich-	ael	row	the	boat	a-	shore	Hal-	ley	loooo	yah
4	5	6	5	6	6	6	5	6	6	6
O	O	O	O	O	I	O	O	O	I	O

•	•	••		•	•	••	•	•	••	••	••
Mich-	ael	row	the	boat	a-	shore	Hal-	ley	loo	hoo	yah
5	6	6	5	5	5	4	4	4	5	4	4
O	O	O	O	I	O	I	O	I	O	I	O

- **"On Top Of Old Smokey"**: An Appalachian favorite.

•	•	•	•	•••	•••••	•	•	•	•	•••• ••••
On	top	of	Old	Smo-	key	all	cov-	ered	with	snow
4	4	5	6	7	6	6	5	6	6	6
O	O	O	O	O	I	I	I	O	I	O

•	•	•	•	•••	•••••	•	•	•	•	•••• ••••
I	lost	my	true	lov-	er	a	court-	in	too	slow
4	4	5	6	6	4	5	5	5	4	4
O	O	O	O	O	I	O	I	O	I	O

• Now Try *Beethoven's Ninth Symphony (the "Ode to Joy")*. Play it chordy, rich and slow. It's very easy, but in a few places you must play notes on the upbeat. Listen while reading the Harptab™ a few times before playing.

5̈	**5̇**	**6̇**	**6̇**	**5̇**	**5̇**	**4̇**	**4̇**	**4̇**	**4̇**	**5̇**	**5̇**	**4̈**
O	I	O	O	I	O	I	O	O	I	O	O	I

5̈	**5̇**	**6̇**	**6̇**	**5̇**	**5̇**	**4̇**	**4̇**	**4̇**	**4̇**	**5̇**	**4̈**	**4̈**
O	I	O	O	I	O	I	O	O	I	O	I	O

4̈	**5̇**	**4̇**	**4̇**	**5̇**	**5̇**	**5̇**	**4̇**	**4̇**	**5̇**	**5̇**	**5̇**	**4̇**	**4̇**	**4̇**	**3̇**
I	O	O	I	O	I	O	O	I	O	I	O	I	O	I	O

5̈	**5̇**	**6̇**	**6̇**	**5̇**	**5̇**	**4̇**	**4̇**	**4̇**	**4̇**	**5̇**	**4̈**	**4̇**	**4̈**
O	I	O	O	I	O	I	O	O	I	O	I	O	O

The Minor Scale

As I discussed in the "Alphabets of Music" section (page 8), the Minor Scale is the alphabet of certain types of folk music. It is most easily played between 6 In and 10 In. Try it left to right, then right to left.

6	7	7	8	8	9	9	10
In	In	Out	In	Out	In	Out	In

Single High Notes

Single high notes may be a little more difficult to get clearly than single low or middle notes. If you have problems, play more softly, concentrate on being *exactly centered* over the desired note, and work on Getting Serious About Single Noting (page 32).

Minor Scale Songs

Re-read the directions for playing Major Scale songs on page 27 if you need to, then try this lovely Minor song. *Greensleeves* has been slightly simplified, to avoid the use of bending. If you like the plaintive sound of the Minor Scale, be sure to work out *Summertime*, below.

• *"Greensleeves"*: A Minor Scale classic.

A-	las	my	lo-	ve	you	do	me	wro	ng	to	cast	me	o
6	7	8	8	9	8	8	7	6	6	7	7	6	6
I	O	I	O	I	O	I	I	O	I	I	O	I	I

out	dis	court	eous	ly		For	I	do	love	you	with	all	my
6	6	7	6	5		6	7	8	8	9	8	8	7
O	I	I	O	O		I	O	I	O	I	O	I	I

hea	rt	and	who	but	my	la	a	dy	Green	sleeves.
6	6	7	7	7	6	6	5	6	6	6
O	I	I	O	I	I	O	O	O	I	I

How To Figure Out Songs For Yourself

It's not too hard to figure out how to play the rest of a song once you know the first few notes, or even the first note. You can practice this by working out the rest of these song fragments below. They are all based on the Major Scale, unless otherwise mentioned, and notated for first position playing. It may help to practice playing the Major Scale (page 26) a few times before working on the song fragment.

Play the portion of the song that I've written out for you a few times. You may be able to find the next note or two by momentum — just keep going! If that doesn't work, think about that next note, the one that's not written down. Do you think that it's a higher note or a lower note than the last one? Start experimenting, and if you hit a note that sounds right, write it down. By a process of trial and error, you'll eventually come up with all the notes!

The more you play, the easier this will become, so don't worry if you can't seem to do it at first. Just come back to these fragments later on, and work them out one by one.

• *Taps* is an easy one to start with — all Out notes. Then try *Amazing Grace*, which uses the holes between 6 and 10.

Day	is	Done		A	maz	ing	grace
3	3	4		6	7	8	8
O	O	O		O	O	O	O

• *Twinkle Twinkle* stays in the middle of the harp. So does *Red River Valley,* if you begin the last line on the note 6 In, which you will have to do to avoid the need to bend.

Twin	kle	twin	kle		From	this	val	ley
4	4	6	6		3	4	5	5
O	O	O	O		O	O	O	O

• And finally, here's a Minor Scale section or lick similar to one used in the **Rolling Stone's** *Miss You*. This lick is derived from an old Minor Scale song called *Lovely Joan*.

•	•	•	•	•	•	•
6	**8**	**7**	**6**	**6**	**6**	
I	I	O	I	O	I	

• Now that you've practiced working from a fragment, try figuring out a song that everybody knows from the first note alone! *Happy Birthday* is Major based, and all the notes located between holes 6 and 9. It begins on 6 Out, and requires a quick octave jump from the 6 Out to 9 Out at one point — a good thing to know how to do for blues, too!

How To Figure Out Hits From The Sixties

Here are some more recent famous songs that you can practice figuring out from the first note! I've chosen some of my favorite '60's hits. This is a very good exercise for training your ears to pick out the notes of a scale that are used in a particular song.

Choose a song that you know very well, play the Major Scale (or Minor Scale, if I have indicated it) a few times for a warm-up, then see if you can locate the second note. And the third. And so on!

• **Bob Dylan** was my early harmonica role model, and his *Blowin' In The Wind,* which begins on 6 Out, was the first song that I learned to play. *Mr. Tambourine Man,* which begins on 7 Out, followed.

• **Gershwin's** *Summertime*, more recently popularized by the late, lamented **Janis Joplin**, is based on the Minor Scale. It begins on 8 Out, and all notes can be found between holes number 8 and 5, so the notes 6 Out and 5 In must be added to the Minor Scale on page 29, which you should practice before attempting this most beautiful of American songs.

• Another of my favorite **Janis Joplin** tunes, *Mercedes Benz*, begins with a 4 Out to 6 Out jump, just like *Twinkle Twinkle Little Star* does, although the timing is different.

• The main verse of **Crosby, Stills, Nash & Young's** poignant *Teach Your Children* is simple to play, and begins on repeated 5 Out notes. How many? You figure it out!

• *Puff The Magic Dragon* and *Leaving On A Jet Plane*, both popularized by **Peter, Paul and Mary,** are Major Scale tunes. The first begins on 7 Out, the second on 4 Out.

• *The Night They Drove Old Dixie Down*, by **The Band,** is characteristic of the mournful sound of the Minor Scale, and begins on the first note of that scale, 6 In.

• **Simon and Garfinkel's** *59th Street Bridge Song* (which I remember as "'Slow Down..."), is Major Scale based although it begins on the somewhat unusual note 6 In. Their *Scarborough Fair* is Minor-based, and begins on 4 In.

Getting Serious About Single Noting

As I said back on page 7:
- The Single Hole Mouth requires crimping or puckering of the lips.

- It's the mouth shape you use when whistling, or drinking through a straw.

- Your upper lip should be curling up towards your nose, like a dog snarling, rather than curving down to cover your upper front teeth like a camel sneering.

- And try to keep your throat and tongue relaxed, even though your lip muscles may feel somewhat tense at first.

Here are some additional tips:
- Make sure that your upper lip is well on top of the harmonica, and your lower lip well under it. Pout your lips way out, as though you were trying to kiss someone who was just a bit too far away, then push the harp way in.

- It should be the wet inner part of your lips that touch the harp, not the dry outer part.

- Your lips form a complete circle of muscle tissue — get used to the feeling of contracting that muscular ring both from top to bottom (which probably feels more familiar) *and* from **side to side**.

- Use a mirror to practice making the single hole mouth position as pictured on page 7.

- **Practice** on holes 1 and 10 at first, they are the easiest. **Listen** so that you can hear when you get a single note, and when you don't.

- **Don't get discouraged. Keep on practicing, and use a wider mouth for now.**

Relaxing With 2 In

For many of you, 2 In won't be much of a problem. Five or ten minutes of practice with this section and you'll have a clean, controllable 2 In, and be able to begin using it. So I don't want to scare anyone about it, even though it was frustrating for me, for a while (because I didn't have a *teacher*, like you do, and didn't realize that it was a problem caused by the harmonica, and not by me).

2 In is a very important note in **Second Position**. Since, for many folk, it can be a bit harder to get a clear sound out of 2 In than other notes, it's time to work on it.

Cover the holes 1, 2, and 3 with your mouth. Breathe out, softly. As soon as you begin to feel even slightly empty, slow your exhale down to nothing. Begin to inhale with tremendous delicacy, taking care to keep your throat and mouth relaxed and very open. If you're lucky, you'll be rewarded with a clear, mellow sounding 123 In chord.

If your 123 In sounds rather like the barking of a sick seal, then you need to work on relaxing the inside of your mouth, since **tightness** is what makes this note sound bad! The following points will help.

• Make sure that your mouth is a **full three holes wide.** It's easier to work on 2 In without having to worry about single noting.

• **Keep your mouth as wide open as possible inside,** as though you had a big mouthful of water.

• Your teeth should be **far enough apart** to be out of the air stream.

• Your tongue should be lying relaxed in the bottom of your mouth, **free of tension,** like a sea cucumber lolling on the bottom of the ocean.

• If your 2 In is still sounding sick, try keeping your **nose open** while you inhale. Doing so tends to relax the inside of your mouth.

• **Be patient, relax, and keep on going.** Just return to this page and your work on the elusive 2 In every so often. The "barky" 2 In is good pre-bending practice, anyways!

The Train

Everybody likes to hear a harmonica sound like a train, and it's a great exercise for your 123 chord. Satisfy your breathing needs through the harmonica. That means if you begin feeling too empty, play your inhales harder and your exhales softer. Give this one a try!

•	•	•	•	•	•	•	•	•	•	•	•
123	123	123	123	123	123	123	123	123	123	123	123
I	I	O	O	I	I	O	O	I	I	O	O

Add an articulation to the Out chords for a more exciting train. I like to use "chugga". Emphasize the downbeat, "chug":

	chugga	chugga			chugga	chugga			chugga	chugga	
•	•	•	•	•	•	•	•	•	•	•	•
123	123	123	123	123	123	123	123	123	123	123	123
I	I	O	O	I	I	O	O	I	I	O	O

And if you're *really* adventurous, try a chugga articulation on the In chords as well. But try to keep your mouth relaxed, since articulation on the 2 In can tend to tense up your tone, if you're not careful!

The Hand Wah Wah

To produce the Hand Wah Wah effect, hold the harmonica in your left hand as pictured on page ##, and use your right to form a cup behind it. As you open and close the cup, the sound quality changes. The more airtight your cup is, the more you can change the sound. It's rather like making the war whoop of the Hollywood Indian (real Native Americans never actually did it). Keep the following in mind:

• Left hand fingers out straight and tightly together (no gaps between them).

• Base of right thumb is next to left thumb.

• Wrists close together.

• Bend right hand down at wrist to open cup.

• Do it in front of a mirror to make sure that the cup is actually opening and closing.

• Practice drinking water from your hands to develop a good cup.

• Once the cup feels comfortable, and your right wrist is under control, you can wah wah *any* rhythm patterns in this book, as I demonstrate.

All Aboard: Whistlin' The Train

Now that you've got a good wheel clackin' train, what else do ya need? Right: a whistle. Use the <u>45</u> In chord for a whistle, then throw in a few special effects as discussed below. Exhale plenty on those beats of silence after each whistle, or you'll be too full to handle the next In chords.

•	•	•	•	•	•	•	•	•••	•	•••	•
<u>123</u>	<u>123</u>	<u>123</u>	<u>123</u>	<u>123</u>	<u>123</u>	<u>123</u>	<u>123</u>	<u>45</u>		<u>45</u>	
I	I	O	O	I	I	O	O	I		I	

•	•	•	•	•	•	•	•	•••	•	•••	•
<u>123</u>	<u>123</u>	<u>123</u>	<u>123</u>	<u>123</u>	<u>123</u>	<u>123</u>	<u>123</u>	<u>45</u>		<u>45</u>	
I	I	O	O	I	I	O	O	I		I	

Once you feel comfortable with the breathing and timing of the train and whistle, try a hand wah wah during the three beats of each whistle. Or try a 4 to 5 shake, if you're beginning to get a handle on single notes, or even an **"Oy Yoy Yoy"**, below.

And make that train real. Is it coming towards you? It gets louder. Going away? Gets softer, 'til all you can hear is the whistle, fading out in the distance. Leaving the station? It starts slow and loud, and picks up speed as it fades away. Coming into the station? It gets louder and slower. If you're on the train, the sound level stays the same, though the speed may change. But if you're laying under the bridge drinkin' Sterno the train speed is constant, but the sound begins with a lonesome whistle far away, gets intolerably loud, then vanishes into the countryside...

We'll do lots more with the train, in Volume Two.

Try an **"Oy yoy yoy" articulation.** Simply whisper **"Oy yoy yoy"** through the 45 In. Exaggerate the tongue motion of each "oy" and "yoy" by widening your tongue, and flattening its sides between your teeth. **This articulation will later help with** *bending*, **so it's worth a moment.**

And now — back to the blues!

Where the Blues Began

I'm not gonna try to describe the blues to you. If you're human, you've felt 'em already. Because the type of music we call the blues expresses feelings — and everybody has feelings.

There are optimistic blues and pessimistic blues. Self-congratulatory blues and self-destructive blues. The lonely blues, the poor blues, the metaphysical blues, the Cadillac-won't-start blues. Different events have different effects on different people. One person's stubbed toe is another's major catastrophe — and vice versa. But everyone has feelings, and thus both the right and reason to play the blues.

What I want to do now is to give you enough historical and structural knowledge of the blues to let you play your own, so let's jump over to Europe and Africa, a thousand years ago.

Now, ever since emerging from the Dark Ages, the upper-class European musical tradition (as opposed to the folk, or lower-class tradition) had one major priority. That was to be able to exactly notate and reproduce any specific piece of music, with no room for deviation or personal interpretation. Thus the musical notation system now known as "standard notation" and the harpsichord and eventually the piano were developed. The Major and Minor Scales were used almost exclusively.

On the other continent, the Africans had a sophisticated musical tradition, but not much of a technological tradition. Thus they lacked pianos, and had no written notation system. Their music was more personal and interpretive, and often improvised. Favorite songs were passed on by mouth, changing from singer to singer, and changing over time. The rhythms and beats of a piece of music were considered more important, and were more rigidly adhered to, than any exactly repeated use of particular scale notes (as was the case in Europe).

A scale similar to the modern Blues Scale was probably used, but with the flexibility to change notes or leave notes out, as each singer desired. When the Africans were kidnapped over to the "New World" (new to Europe, that is) their music was one of the few traditions that they were able to bring with them. So the unwritten, spontaneous, personalized African musical tradition merged, mingled, and miscegenated with the structured, rigid, notated European musical tradition — giving birth to The Blues!

Somewhere, somehow, in the region where the Mississippi River runs into the Gulf of Mexico, a new musical style emerged, based on the use of what we now call the Blues Scale, combined with a particular chord structure known as the Blues Structure.

No one now alive knows exactly when or where it all began. But this new style of music was so striking and expressive that it quickly spread from hamlet to hamlet, from town to town, and from city to city. It is now the most widespread musical style, and the most widely used chord structure, that the world has ever known!

The Twelve Bar Blues Structure

What do the Batman TV show theme song, The Beatles, and B. B. King have in common? You guessed it: the Twelve Bar Blues! Most blues, much rock and roll, and lots of funk, soul and jazz songs are based on this structure.

As you no doubt remember, chord structures are repeated patterns of two or more chords, like the four bar D Minor/C Major structure from page 22. Here is what you need to know about the Blues Structure:

• The Twelve Bar Blues Structure is constructed of **3 different chords** that are stacked together in a particular order.

• Each Twelve Bar Chord Structure is called one **verse**. A typical blues song is made up of from three to eight verses.

• Each of these chords has a name, which you might consider it's "generic" name. **Please memorize these three chord names, and don't worry about what they mean.** They are very old names, dating to the middle ages, and their meanings are almost lost in antiquity. However, these names are useful labels for each chord:

Tonic Chord   Subdominant Chord   Dominant Chord

• From now on, most of the information in the book is pretty important. At least make sure that you read every • bulleted line.

• A **turnaround** is three or four beats of Dominant note or chord thrown in as part of the end of the Third Tonic Phrase's 8 beats. The turnaround "announces" that one verse is ending, and another is about to begin.

• A blues song often begins with an **introduction.** An introduction is usually four bars long, and is usually structured exactly like the last four bars of a regular verse: Dominant, Subdominant, Tonic and Turnaround.

Look at the Blues Structure Chart below while you listen to me describe a Twelve Bar Blues in words, and to my musical demonstration of two Twelve Bar Blues verses. Notice how the second verse starts right after the first one ends, and how both have exactly the same structure as shown on the chart.

You've probably heard this exact structure thousands of times. Why is it so popular? Why does this particular musical framework seem to grab people on a gut level? I can't answer those questions — but since I first heard the blues, I've been a believer!

Spend some time here. Relax, close your eyes, turn the volume up, tap your foot and let these Twelve Bar "changes" sink into your very soul...

Section of Blues	Bars	Beats
First Tonic	4	16
First Subdominant	2	8
Second Tonic	2	8
Dominant	1	4
Second Subdominant	1	4
Third Tonic (includes Turnaround)	2	8
Total	12	48

Taking a Position... *Second Position*

Up until now, we've been doing our most interesting improvising work in Third Position. I love Third Position, and play it daily, but **Second Position** (also known as **Cross Harp**) is actually both more versatile and more commonly used with the Twelve Bar Blues Structure.

This means that I hope you've been working on getting a good, clear **2 In**. If not, go to page 32 for some 2 In review. Third Position Blues will be covered in great detail in Volume Two, and in my Positions Tape.

Harpin' The Blues

We'll begin by playing a very simple **Second Position Twelve Bar Blues Structure.** We'll use only the notes that sound rightest with the Tonic, Subdominant, and Dominant Chords. Soon we'll add some tense notes, for more exciting playing, but for right now I just want you to get the feel of the Twelve Bar Blues Chord *Structure* itself.

When using a C harmonica in Second Position, G will be our Tonic, C our Subdominant, and D our Dominant (and turnaround) notes. We'll produce these notes by using the following holes:

In Second Position:

- **Tonic = 2 In   Subdominant = 4 Out   Dominant = 4 In**

If possible, use **single notes** when playing this Blues Structure. If you can't, use <u>123</u> **In** for the Tonic Chord, <u>345</u> **Out** for Subdominant, and <u>45</u> **In** for the Dominant and turnaround.

Pre-Blues Practice

Practice the 2 In to 4 Out jump, like this. Memorize that distance with your hand:

••••	••••	••••	••••	••••	••••	••••	••••
2	4	2	4	2	4	2	4
In	Out	In	Out	In	Out	In	Out

Now practice the 4 In to 4 Out to 2 In sequence, using a Dirty Dirty Dog rhythm. I haven't written out all the "dirtys" and "dogs" — but I hope you've memorized it by now. Don't forget the beat of silence. You'll need it to breathe during.

••••	••••	••••	••••	••••	••••	••••	••••
4	4	2	2	4	4	2	2
In	Out	In	In	In	Out	In	In

Lastly, practice this Third Tonic with turnaround:

•	•	•	•	•	•	•	•
Dirty	Dirty	Dog		Dirty	Dog	Dog	
2	2	2		2	4	4	
I	I	I		I	I	I	

Well, you've practiced all the parts of the **Second Position Twelve Bar Blues Structure.** It's time to put them all together. Try it with a Dirty Dirty Dog articulation throughout, but use the above Third Tonic with turnaround. Ready? No introduction, just 1 2 3 4!

First Tonic

• • • • • • • • • • • • • • • •
2 2 2   2 2 2   2 2 2   2 2 2
I I I   I I I   I I I   I I I

First Subdominant   **Second Tonic**

• • • • • • • • • • • • • • • •
4 4 4   4 4 4   2 2 2   2 2 2
O O O   O O O   I I I   I I I

Dominant   **Subdominant**   **Third Tonic**   **Turnaround**

• • • • • • • • • • • • • • • •
4 4 4   4 4 4   2 2 2   2 4 4
I I I   O O O   I I I   I I I

Play this Twelve Bar at least a dozen times now, both along with my backing music and solo. You might enjoy going to the Second Position backing music at the end of side two of the tape and playing a longer series of these blues verses.

The Second Position Jamm Rule

Just as I devised simple rules for First Position (any Out notes) and Third Position (any 4 through 10 In notes), there's one for **Second Position** as well: **1 through 5 In.**
Try a 16 beat Dirty Dirty Dog pattern down there:

• • • • • • • • • •
Dirty   Dirty   Dog   Dada   Dada   Da
<u>123</u>   <u>123</u>   <u>34</u>   <u>123</u>   <u>123</u>   <u>1</u>
I   I   I   I   I   I

   • • • • • • • •
   Dirty   Dirty   Ding   Dong   Dog
   <u>123</u>   <u>123</u>   <u>34</u>   <u>34</u>   <u>2</u>
   I   I   I   I   I

Here's a new Third Tonic with turnaround which substitutes 1 In (a D note) for the 4 In (also a D) that you used in your first Second Position Twelve Bar: We'll use this, and the following turnarounds, in just a moment.

•	•	•	•	•	•	•	•
Dirty	Dirty	Ding	Dong	Dog			
<u>123</u>	<u>123</u>	<u>34</u>	<u>34</u>	2	1	1	
I	I	I	I	I	I	I	

Practice this sliding turnaround. It's one bar long, and can be added to the the first bar of any Third Tonic. Notice the notation that indicates a slide from 5 In to 1 In. The slide turnaround at right is simply tacked on to a first bar of 2 In. The one at left is added to a more complex one bar lick (and one which will require lots of breath, so start empty)

2	2	3	4	5╲1	1		2	2	2	5╲1	1
I	I	I	I	I I	I		I	I	I	I I	I

Now spend a moment experimenting with the Simple Second Position Jamm Rule of 1 through 5 In. Apply any of the slides, jumps, and rhythms that you've been using all along, to these 1 through 5 In notes to make up some cross harp licks of your own.

The "Dwah" Articulation

Here's another "pre-bending" effect. Simply whisper a clear **"Dwah"** through your <u>34</u> In. Thinking of it as a **"Doo ah"** may be easier at first. This articulation is most often used on either <u>34</u> In or <u>45</u> In. Try it on the <u>34</u> In's of the Dirty Dog licks just above, for a bluesy sound.

Jamm Rules and the Twelve Bar Blues

Amazingly enough, we find that in the Second Position Twelve Bar Blues we can use our First, Second, and Third Position Jamm Rules to create entire improvised verses. Simply apply the three rules, adding a turnaround at the end of the Third Tonic. The Visualization and Relaxation exercise in Appendix C may help you just let the music flow out, as you play either solo or along with my backing music.

The Simple Jamming Rules

- **All Tonic Portions: Use 1 through 5 In**

- **All Subdominant Portions: Use 1 through 10 Out**

- **All Dominant Portions (and turnaround): Use 4 through 10 In**

Listen to my example of a *Sliding Blues*. I'll simply slide around through the entire Twelve Bar, using a rhythm pattern more or less based on the 16 beat Dirty Dirty Dog rhythm, with a 5 In to 1 In turnaround.

Thematic Twelve Bar Jamming

It's also easy to take a rhythm pattern that you know, and apply it throughout a Twelve Bar. This is called thematic jamming, since one theme is carried (with some broken expectations, of course) throughout the verse.

Do this just by memorizing the **motions** that your **tongue** makes (articulations), and the **motions** that your **hand** makes (low to high, high to middle, hole 4 to hole 5, etc.). Simply use these same motions on 1 through 5 In for all Tonics, 1 through 10 Out for all Subdominants, and 4 through 10 In for all Dominants or turnarounds. Use 1 In for a great turnaround, as well.

Here's a Twelve Bar that uses the 16 beat Up and Down Dog Lick as it's theme, with broken expectations during the second subdominant.

```
 •   •   •   •   •   •   •   •   •   •   •   •   •   •   •   •
 2   2   34      2   2   1       2   2   34  34  2
 I   I   I       I   I   I       I   I   I   I   I

 •   •   •   •   •   •   •   •   •   •   •   •   •   •   •   •
 4   4   5       4   4   3       2   2   34  34  2
 O   O   O       O   O   O       I   I   I   I   I

 •   •   •   •   •   •   •   •   •   •   •   •   •   •   •   •
 4   4   5       slide out       2   2   34  34  2   1   1
 I   I   I       O   O   O        I   I   I   I   I   I   I
```

Try applying some other rhythm patterns or licks as themes throughout a Twelve Bar, using my Simple Jamm Rules.

The Ins and Outs of Second Position

Just as both In and Out notes can be used in Third Position, even though the Third Position Jamm Rule says 4 through 10 In only, Out notes can also be used sprinkled in with the 1 through 5 In notes of Second Position licks.

The exact same breathing rhythms that we used to incorporate Out notes into Third Position can be used with the 1 through 5 In Jamm Rule. Try it through the <u>123</u> In and <u>123</u> Out chord. Then do it moving around in different ways from 1 to 5.

•	•	•	•	•	•	•	•
Dirty	Dirty	Dog		Dirty	Dirty	Dog	
In Out	In Out	In		In Out	In Out	In	

•	•	•	•	•	•	•	•
Dirty	Dirty	Dirty	Dirty	Dirty	Dirty	Dog	
In Out	In Out	In Out	In Out	In Out	In Out	In	

One of my favorites is written out below. As always, use it as an example, but don't worry about copying the exact notes.

•	•	•	•	•	•	•	•
Dirty	Dirty	Dog		Dirty	Dirty	Dog	
5 5	4 4	3		5 5	4 4	3	
In Out	In Out	In		In Out	In Out	In	

•	•	•	•	•	•	•	•
Dirty	Dirty	Dirty	Dirty	Dirty	Dirty	Dog	
5 5	4 4	3 3	1 2	2 3	3 3	4	
In Out	In Out	In Out	In Out	In Out	In Out	In	

An Easy In and Out Way To Play A Twelve Bar

The fact is that the Second position In and Out licks can be used throughout a Twelve Bar, so long as there is background music to help indicate the chord changes. Some of you will find this easy. But for others, it will seem too shapeless, since the Tonic and Subdominant parts will not be clearly different.

Give my taped example a listen, and try it if you like. This is all you need to do.

- Choose an In and Out breathing rhythm that you like.

- Use it with the 1 In through 5 In notes for eight bars (to form the First Tonic, First Subdominant, and Second Tonic).

- Use it with the 4 In through 10 In notes for two bars (to form the Dominant and Second Subdominant).

- Then return to the 1 through 5 In notes for two bars, including a 1 In, or a 4 through 10 In turnaround (to form the Third Tonic with turnaround).

If this style of playing appeals to you, do it along with my Second Position play-along music at the end of the cassette's side two. It works well with the "Playing From The Gut" exercise, since it doesn't require much thinking!

In The Style Of Mr. Bob Dylan

Here are a few of the general types of licks that my first harmonica hero uses in his recordings. There are some harp players who would say that Mr. Dylan is not a great blues harpist. Yet I would call him a *virtuoso*, as his amazingly inventive if unconventional playing, along with his lyric mastery, had power enough to arouse an entire generation.

These are Second Position licks based on the Blues Scale, and if you've practiced your Oy Yoy Yoy train whistle effect (page 35), and your Little Walter lick timing (as described by Dog notation below), they will be easy. Try this eight beater. Note the anticipated timing on the 45 Out note. It occurs during the upbeat and lasts for a beat and a half.

Dog	Dog	Dirtyyyyyyyy		Dog				
Oy	Yoy	Yoy						
45	45	45	45	3				
I	I	I	O	I				

Try a sixteen beat version that uses the first bar above twice, then the entire two bars once. The notes in parentheses are for a turnaround, in case you use this lick at the end of a Twelve Bar.

Oy	Yoy	Yoy		Oy	Yoy	Yoy	
45	45	45	45	45	45	45	45
I	I	I	O	I	I	I	O

Continued on following page

Oy	Yoy	Yoy					
•	•	•	•	•	•	•	•
<u>45</u>	<u>45</u>	<u>45</u>	<u>45</u>	3	(1)	(1)	
I	I	I	O	I	(I)	(I)	

For an exciting Dylan style Twelve Bar, play four of the eight beaters, then one of the 16 beaters, with two extra beats of 1 In for a turnaround.

John Lennon Style Jamming

Like Bob Dylan, the late and cruelly missed John Lennon was a great musician, if not a great blues harpist. But whatever he played fit in well, as did this lick similar to the ones used in the Beatles song **"I Should Have Known Better"**. John repeated a lick of this type throughout the song, sometimes as a four beater, and sometimes as a 16 beater. He used both a **shake** and an **Oy Yoy** type articulation on the <u>45</u> Ins.

Here's a 16 beater, made up of two four beaters plus an eight beater. Use a "Dwah" on the <u>34</u> In, if you like. Three of these fit into a blues verse.

Oy	Yoy			Oy	Yoy		
•	•	•	•	•	•	•	•
<u>45</u> www	<u>45</u> www	<u>56</u>	<u>56</u>	<u>56</u>	<u>45</u> www	<u>45</u> www	<u>56</u> <u>56</u> <u>56</u>
I	I	O	I	O	I	I	O I O

Oy	Yoy			
•	•	•	•	
<u>45</u> www	<u>45</u> www	<u>45</u>	<u>45</u>	<u>45</u>	<u>34</u>
I	I	O	I	O	I

A Classical Twelve Bar

This is a thematic Twelve Bar Blues based on the **John Mayall** and **Sonny Boy Williamson II** eight beat lick on page 24.

Practice the main lick using the <u>123</u> chord. Emphasize that last In!:

•	•		•	•		•	•	•	•		•
<u>123</u>	<u>123</u>	<u>123</u>	<u>123</u>	<u>123</u>	<u>123</u>	<u>123</u>	<u>123</u>	<u>123</u>	<u>123</u>		
In	In	Out	In	In	Out	In	In	Out	In!		

Then work on this Subdominant version. Practice the breathing rhythm first, then use the <u>45</u> Out and <u>34</u> In chords.

•	•	•	•	•	•	•	•	•	•	•	•
Out	Out	In	Out	Out	In	Out	Out	In	Out!		

•   •   •   •   •   •   •   •

<u>45</u> <u>45</u>   <u>34</u>   <u>45</u> <u>45</u>   <u>34</u>   <u>45</u> <u>45</u>   <u>34</u> <u>45!</u>

O O   I   O O   I   O O   I O

And here's the Dominant (which uses a "Dwah-Dah" articulation) and Second Subdominant (which is mostly silent):

Dwah   Dwahdah Dwahdah Dwahdah

•   •   •   •   •   •   •   •

<u>45</u>   <u>45</u> <u>45</u>   <u>45</u> <u>45</u>   <u>45</u> <u>45</u>   <u>45</u>

In   In In   In In   In In   Out

Put all the pieces together for an exciting blues harp verse, reminiscent of Mayall's *Room To Move.* This verse, like some others, has no turnaround at all.

•   •   •   •   •   •   •   •

<u>123</u> <u>123</u>   <u>123</u>   <u>123</u> <u>123</u>   <u>123</u>   <u>123</u> <u>123</u>   <u>123</u> <u>123</u>

In In   Out   In In   Out   In In   Out In!

•   •   •   •   •   •   •   •

<u>123</u> <u>123</u>   <u>123</u>   <u>123</u> <u>123</u>   <u>123</u>   <u>123</u> <u>123</u>   <u>123</u> <u>123</u>

In In   Out   In In   Out   In In   Out In!

•   •   •   •   •   •   •   •

<u>45</u> <u>45</u>   <u>34</u>   <u>45</u> <u>45</u>   <u>34</u>   <u>45</u> <u>45</u>   <u>34</u> <u>45!</u>

OutOut   In   OutOut   In   OutOut   In Out

•   •   •   •   •   •   •   •

<u>123</u> <u>123</u>   <u>123</u>   <u>123</u> <u>123</u>   <u>123</u>   <u>123</u> <u>123</u>   <u>123</u> <u>123</u>

In In   Out   In In   Out   In In   Out In!

Dwah   Dwahdah Dwahdah Dwahdah

•   •   •   •   •   •   •   •

<u>45</u>   <u>45</u> <u>45</u>   <u>45</u> <u>45</u>   <u>45</u> <u>45</u>   <u>45</u>

In   In In   In In   In In   Out

•   •   •   •   •   •   •   •

<u>123</u> <u>123</u>   <u>123</u>   <u>123</u> <u>123</u>   <u>123</u>   <u>123</u> <u>123</u>   <u>123</u> <u>123</u>

In In   Out   In In   Out   In In   Out In!

If you're really hot on rhythm, you can even substitute the Tequila rhythm pattern for the Mayall rhythm pattern. Just use the exact same holes and Ins and Outs for a rockin' blues!

•   •   •   •   •   •   •   •

In In   Out Out In In In   Out Out In In   Out Out In

The Blues Scale

Somewhere in the Deep South, perhaps as many as a hundred years ago, an unknown Afro-American musician decided to play some of what would eventually be called blues music on the harmonica. But the Major Scale built into the instrument (from 4 Out to 7 Out) by Mr. Hohner just didn't sound very bluesy.

So our anonymous forefather (or foremother, as the case may have been) discovered an alternate way to produce a bluesier scale. This new scale could be played most easily from 2 In to 6 Out, and required the use of bent notes in two places. We now call this the **Second Position Blues Scale**. It is the most commonly used Blues Scale.

Spend some time listening to my repeated *Blues Scale Blues*. If you want to refresh your memory on the theory of the Blues Scale, the alphabet of blues music, read page 8 and Appendix B.

Bending

Bending is the most important of the advanced blues harmonica techniques. It requires a good ability to get single notes, and lots of tongue control. The pre-bending effects (like the **Oy Yoy Yoy**, and the **Dwah**) that you've no doubt been practicing will help you to bend, but I'm not going to cover bending in detail in this book.

I've learned from my students that it just doesn't pay to try to teach bending too early. However, not to worry, because I've devoted an entire 90 minute cassette and booklet to the subject (see page 60-62), as well as a considerable portion of Volume Two of this series.

Bending involves using the tongue to partially block the airway while playing one or two notes, which causes the reeds to vibrate more slowly, and the pitch of the note to lower. On some notes, like 1, 4, 5, and 6 In, there is only one available degree of bentness. 2 In has two possible degrees of bentness, one lower than the other, and 3 In has three. In my bending notation, the height of the little "b" in relationship to the O or I tells you how deeply to bend the note. The bent notes of the following scale are bent to the least possible degree. The 4 In can be bent no further, but the 3 In can be.

The Second Position Blues Scale

2	3	4	4	4	5	6
I	I^b	O	I^b	I	I	O

Fortunately for beginners, many Blues Scale notes require no bending, so we can immediately begin to create Blues Scale licks. As you can guess by looking at the Blues Scale, the pre-bending **Oy Yoy Yoy** that we use on the <u>45</u> In works so well because it begins to bend the 4 In, and the **Dwah** on 34 In sounds bluesy because it partially bends the 3 In.

The Simplified Second Position Blues Scale

Although a Blues Scale without bends lacks soul, playing this simplified version will help us when we reach the real thing in Volume Two. Play it a few times, from left to right, and from right to left (which I prefer).

•	•	•	•	•	•
2	**3**	**4**	**4**	**5**	**6**
I	**I**	**O**	**I**	**I**	**O**

Soon you'll be using this entire scale in a blues, but right now I'll show you a few famous licks that can be played using only a few Blues Scale notes at a time.

The *I'm A (Wo)Man* Type Lick

Variations on this famous lick are used in many blues songs. It begins with an anticipation, on an upbeat. When counting down before songs that begin on anticipated notes, instead of our usual 1234 count, we often count 123. Say the timing a few times, maybe practice your 2 In to 4 Out jump if you think you need to, and go for it!

•	•	•	•	•	•	•	•
Da	Dir	ty	Dog		Da	Dir	ty	Dog

•	•	•	•	•	•	•	•
2	4	3	2		2	4	3	2
I	O	I	I		I	O	I	I

If you like, you can sing in the two beats of silence, as I do! Or *sandwich* in a lick, as described below and on tape.

The *Hoochie Coochie* Type Lick

Once again, here's a lick that's been used in many songs, including the one whose name I've labelled it with. It begins on an upbeat, and requires clear single noting. Two notes occur during one of the upbeats, as indicated in the timing.

Da Didely Dog   Da Didely Dog

4 5 4 5 6   4 5 4 5 6
I I I I O   I I I I O

It's good to make use of silence in your playing. But if those two beat silences start feeling empty (and you haven't learned to sing the blues yet, which of course is more Volume Two material) use a *sandwich* lick.

The Sandwich Lick

The sandwich lick is anything that you sandwich into those above beats of silence. If you like, you can actually sandwich them into each other, which sounds pretty good and is a great exercise in timing.

2 4 3   2   4 5 4 5 6   2 4 3   2   4 5 4 5 6
I O I   I   I I I I O   I O I   I   I I I I O

Another more generic sandwich that I like to use is simply any Second Position Jamm Rule lick (1 through 5 In), as I demonstrated with the I'm A Man (or I'm A Woman) lick on the cassette.

Blues Scale Blues

If you've practiced the simplified Blues Scale, you can pick and choose notes from it, and play them with timing variations throughout a Twelve Bar, as I did with the unsimplified Blues Scale. Try this bluesy verse if you like, or just make up something similar of your own. Notice how I make extra use of the 4 Out during the Subdominants, and of the 4 and 5 In during the Dominant. And, of course, I tack on a 1 In turnaround.

A Simple Blues Scale Blues Verse

•	•	•	•	•	•	•	•	•	•	•	•	•	•	•	•	•	•
2	3	4		4	5	6		6	5	4	3	2					
I	I	O		I	I	O		O	I	I	I	I					

•	•	•	•	•	•	•	•	•	•	•	•	•	•	•	•
4	4	3	2	4	4	3		2	3	4	4	6			
O	O	I	I	O	O	I		I	I	O	I	O			

•	•		•	•	•	•	•	•
5	5	4	5		4	4	4	6
I	I	I	I		O	O	O	O

•		•		•		•	•		•	•
6	6	5	5	4	4	4	3	2	1	1
O	O	I	I	I	I	O	I	I	I	I

> Note: The typo mentioned on the tape has been corrected in this new printing. Also, please be aware that the timing notation (dots) written here are approximate. Although the notes are accurate, sometimes I hit a note just *before* the actual beat, for added rhythmic interest. The two 4 Out notes in the middle of the second line are a good example of this. Please feel free to experiment with the timing of this verse, yourself!

Putting It All Together

What I've tried to do in this first volume of my *Instant Blues Harmonica* method is to give you some basic techniques, and a variety of ways to use them to make music. You can use what you have learned in many ways.

Some of you will want to stick to a particular way of playing. This might mean specializing in one type of Jamming, like using the Simple Jamm Rules, and playing them along with Twelve Bar backing, or perhaps concentrating on the "In and Out" Jamm Rhythms.

Others of you will want to put all of your techniques together, to create music that integrates the usage of licks, themes, Jamm Rules, and the Blues Scale. I'll give you a few examples of verses like this, but space limitations prevent me from going into this "Hole-istic" harmonica in great detail. However, the "Where To Go From Here" section will provide you with all the resources that you need to continue making the harmonica and the blues your lifelong friends!

Appendix A: "The Musical I.Q. Test"

Dr. Nina S. Feldman is a Princeton-trained developmental psychologist whose skill in experimental design was sharply honed by her work at Educational Testing Services, the designer of most of the nation's standardized tests. But her fascination with quantifying the vagaries of human nature goes back even further, to when she first encountered her twin brother, David Harp! Five years ago, Nina's expertise in the use of self-testing as an educational tool combined with my interest in teaching music to people who considered themselves "unmusical".

Since I began to teach, I had always been dumbfounded by the number of intelligent and competent adults who totally refuse to believe that they could play a musical instrument. Nina, research psychologist that she is, wondered *why* this was.

We devised a 35 question test and began administering it to self-described "musical idiots" and "tonedeaf" folk. Analysis of the test results and interviews with our unmusical "guinea pigs" helped us to isolate what we consider to be the five main causes of musical blockage. A book on the subject is in the works. Following is a simplified version of our "Musical IQ" (Musical Idiot Quotient) self-test.

Are You a Victim of the "Musical Idiot" Syndrome?

How many times in the past few years have you found yourself envying a friend's or performer's musical abilities? Your train of thought may have been, "I wish I could play the guitar like that", followed by "I wish I could play anything like that", then "I wish I could play anything!" and finally "I guess I'm just not very musical".

Do you believe that these talented individuals had the privilege of being born with a natural musical ability? Or that they were "made musical" by having been taught the secrets of music at an early age? Are you privately annoyed that your parents didn't start you on violin or piano lessons when you were five years old? Or perhaps a bit rueful because you did have childhood music lessons that somehow "just didn't take"?

If your answer to any or all of these questions is yes, then you may be a victim of the Musical Idiot Syndrome. Being a "Musical Idiot" simply means that, for whatever reasons, you perceive yourself as being under endowed with musical aptitude or ability. This self-perception has led you to abandon the pursuit of music, although the thought of someday learning to play an instrument is still an active part of your fantasy life. Might you be an "MI"? Then continue reading – help is on the way!

Self-Help for All

The last few years have seen a tremendous upsurge of interest in the topic of self-improvement, and many of our childhood inadequacies have often been resolved with a flourish. Your pear-shaped sixth grade buddy is now training for the Boston Marathon. That painfully shy adolescent cousin is now a business executive and happily "pulling her own strings".

Unfortunately, most self-labeled unmusical folk have not been able to apply these self-improvement techniques to their relationship with making music. This seems to be due to the fact that although an abundance of music instruction exists, the root causes of musical blockage remain largely unexplored. For most musically unfulfilled adults, the problem is not the lack of instruction – it is a lack of belief in their own never-tapped musical ability.

This test is designed to explore your "Musical Idiot Quotient". Although this test is not intended to predict how accomplished a musician you will become, it can help you understand and overcome the areas of musical blockage that have prevented you from realizing your own musical potential. There are no "right" or "wrong" answers in this test. Please answer as honestly as possible by circling any or all answers that apply to you.

Your Musical I.Q.

1. Have you ever felt that it is "too late" for you to be musical?   yes/no

2. Have you ever bought yourself a musical instrument and then not really tried to learn to play it?
   yes   no, always tried   no, never bought one

3. Do you ever look at people who can play some kind of instrument
   and wish that you had that type of talent?   yes/no

4. a). Did you take music lessons as a child?   yes/no
   b). Did you want to take music lessons a a child?   yes/no

5. Imagine yourself feeling an urge to sing. Will you sing:
   Only when alone in the shower, or when driving alone   Only with close friends
   No matter who else is present

6. In elementary school music classes were:
   nonexistent   boring   enjoyable   difficult to understand   frightening

7. Have you ever fantasized about being able to play a musical instrument, even though you never
   actually tried to do it?   yes/no

8. Do you believe that most other people "just kind of pick up" simple instruments like the harmonica
   by themselves?   yes/no

9. If someone placed an instrument in your hands and told you to "make some sounds", would you feel:
   scared   pleased   foolish   excited   upset

10. If you saw an older adult taking beginning music lessons, would it strike you as: somewhat surpris-
    ing   yes/no   somewhat inappropriate   yes/no

The diagnostic value of this test lies not in any total score (which you could use to compare to your friend's score, and brag or complain about) but in the five separate "themes" that your answers will now help you to investigate. In this shortened version of the test two questions relate to each of these five main areas of musical blockage. Please refer back to your answers to the designated questions as you read the following sections. Most people who believe that they are not musical will find that at least a few of these problems apply directly to them.

The Myth of Innate Ability (Refer to Questions 3 and 8)

Many people who foreclose on their own musical potential share a belief in a widespread and damaging musical myth. Do you believe that all musicians are born with innate musical talent? If your answer is yes, you are wrong! Musicians are made, not born! A tremendous body of research exists to verify the fact that musical ability is a near-universal human characteristic that must be nurtured and encouraged.

Once you begin to believe this, you can leave your unmusical self-image behind. Though not all of us may have the energy, dedication or sensitivity to play just like a Segovia or a Jimi Hendrix, the truth of the matter is that anyone with the sincere desire to be musical can learn to play a variety of instruments well.

Ageism: Refer to Questions 1 and 10

Ageism – that is, discrimination against a person based solely on the fact of biological age – is often practiced unconsciously by otherwise well-intentioned people. Prejudiced attitudes against the elderly have become a pervasive but often unadmitted part of our culture. Ageist beliefs may be held by young and old alike, and directed either at others or oneself.

Any person who may eye an untried activity and think wistfully, "I'm too old for that" is an unwitting victim of ageism. An ageist viewpoint holds that "older" people are unlikely to continue to explore any existing talents and incapable of discovering new ones. Music is an ageless pastime! Any holding back that a non-musician might do based on this misguided belief is a sad and unnecessary loss of musical potential.

The next time you find yourself looking askance at the activities of an "elderly" person who is taking some kind of lessons or engaging in a "youthful" pastime, remember that the older adult may be you in 5, 10, or 40 years. Noticing evidence that works against the ageist perspective (which is often promoted by advertising and the media) such as senior citizens re-entering school or taking up a new sport or relationship may lighten your own response to the inevitable aging process.

Actress Billie Burke once remarked, "Age doesn't matter unless you're a cheese." Artist Grandma Moses, pianist Eubie Blake or cellist Pablo Casals would surely have agreed!

Fear of Foolishness (Refer to Questions 5 and 9)

A major problem for many of the "Musical Idiots" whom we have tested is a preoccupation with the question: "What will people think?" Often a seeming fear of failure is actually a fear of ridicule.

Are you afraid that friends or acquaintances would make fun of your attempts to make music? Ask yourself two very important questions: "If I were alone for two months to do as I pleased, how would I really feel about pursuing this?" And, "How do I think other people would react to my doing this?" You may find that you are drawn to learning, but fear that others would disapprove. But remember, regardless of your imagined perceptions of other's reactions, your musical career is only as public as you make it. Many people derive great enjoyment from playing at home, with never an audience at all.

Early Musical Exposure (Questions 4 and 6)

Your early exposure to music may shape the rest of your musical (or non-musical) career. A bad first experience with music can create lasting difficulties. Some of the following are common problems that precipitate a negative attitude towards music. Did your parents force you to take music lessons?

Did Mr. Flutesnoot's music class make your Tuesday mornings miserable throughout grade school? Did an unkind comment on your early playing embarrass you away from further musical self-exposure? Parents, peers, and teachers play an important role in supporting an early love of music. But, the converse is also true. Early discouragement will carry a tremendous impact on a young person's future musicality.

Understanding the effects that early encouragement and discouragement have on you is a crucial part of relinquishing a "Musical Idiot" status. As you peruse your past, tell yourself "What's past is over—*unless* I let it influence me now. Today in the present, I can change my self-image and begin to be musical!" The irascible Ms. Trebleclef from fourth grade has been retired for years, and it's time to get on with business: the business of bringing music into your life!

Approach/Avoidance (Refer to Questions 2, 7 and 9)

These questions can indicate the presence of a common psychological conflict known as approach (wanting very much to be musical) avoidance (fearful of making an attempt to do so). Buying a musical instrument is a strong statement of approach, as is fantasizing about playing. If you do these things but do *not* follow through by actually learning to make music, you may be in the grip of a very strong musical approach/avoidance process.

Sometimes the existence of an approach/avoidance conflict can produce very strong feelings, so if your answer to question 9 included the feelings of scared or upset, or especially combinations like pleased/foolish or excited/upset or scared/excited, you may have an approach/avoidance attitude towards music. Acknowledging an ambivalence towards music can be the first step towards understanding and accepting how this conflict came about, and then resolving it.

Bringing Music Into Your Life

The most common general causes of being unmusical are found amongst the five problem themes described above. No longer can you avoid the real issues by merely saying "I guess I'm just tone-deaf", since no such disease actually exists! If you can hear, you can be musical! There is only one valid reason for your non-musicality: lack of effort or practice.

The only thing that now stands between you and your music is the time and energy necessary to accomplish whatever musical goal you set for yourself. Furthermore, attributing your current lack of musicality to a lack of effort rather than a lack of ability offers you the option of becoming musical whenever you choose to put the effort into doing so. If your goals are realistic ("I will begin to play some guitar" rather than "I must play classical guitar like Segovia") then your success is virtually guaranteed from the outset! All that's necessary is to take a deep breath, turn back to the beginning of this book, and start to play!

Appendix B: Music Theory (For the Musically Insecure)

You don't have to understand music theory in order to make music. But many of my students have found that understanding the "underpinnings" of music has increased their appreciation for the processes involved in the making of music.

I do understand that some of us may feel intimidated by the very idea of music theory (I used to, myself). So I'll try to make my explanations as clear and simple as possible. And I'll start at the very beginning: with the physics of sound.

The Physics of Sound

Picture a pond on a calm, windless day. If you threw a big stone into the center of the pond, it would create ripples that would eventually reach the shore. And if there were a leaf lying at the water's edge, the ripples would move it gently up and down.

Clap your hands, pluck a guitar string, bang on a drum, or blow through the tiny reeds of your harmonica. Many types of physical actions create vibrations that flow invisibly though the air, just as our imaginary stone caused ripples to flow through the water. These vibrations eventually reach a sensitive, leaf-thin membrane inside our heads, called the eardrum. Ripples in the pond will make our leaf move up and down, and these vibrations in the air, caused by vibrating drum head, or guitar strings, or harmonica reed, will make our eardrums move back and forth.

Our eardrums will then be vibrating at the same speed as these air vibrations, and our brain will interpret these eardrum vibrations as a sound which we hear. **The faster the vibration, the higher the sound that our brain tells us we hear. The slower the vibration, the lower the sound.** The wings of a mosquito vibrate very rapidly, and produce a high sound. The muffler of a big Harley-Davidson motorcycle vibrates slowly, and produces a low sound.

Each and every sound, which in music terminology is called a **note**, has its own particular vibrational speed. Our brains can recognize sounds that result from vibrations as slow as 20 vibrations per second (VPS) or as fast as 20,000 VPS. Since the middle ages, each note has been called by a letter name, from A to G.

Most musically untrained people think of sound in a rather vague way. A sound is either "high" or "low". But in reality, sounds are arranged in **"repeated octaves"**. What does that mean? I'll try to explain it clearly and simply. But first, there is one more important fact that we must learn about the vibrations that create sound.

Please consider any particular vibrational speed which produces a sound, like 256 VPS, for example. This note happen to have the letter name of C. If we compare this particular sound, (or "note") with the note produced by 512 VPS (exactly twice as fast, and also called a C note), we'll find that the two sounds seem remarkable alike, although the faster vibration sound is obviously higher.

If we double the speed of vibration once again (1024 VPS, and a C note once again), we find that all three sounds (256 VPS, 512 VPS and 1024 VPS) bear a great similarity to each other. Likewise the sounds produced by 300 VPS, 600 VPS and 1200 VPS sound alike, and so on. Doubling the speed of vibration of a particular sound will always produce a new sound that is very similar to the first one, only higher. We call these similar notes "octave" notes. We can also call the distance between two of these octave notes "one octave".

You can demonstrate this for yourself by blowing out on the number 1, 4, 7, and 10 holes of your harmonica.

Each of these notes will produce a C note, one octave apart.

These octave notes are easier to hear than to describe in words. In fact, even a dog can recognize octave notes. If you train your pooch to expect to be fed when he hears a note of 200 vibrations per second, he'll begin to salivate when he hears a note of 400 vibrations per second as well!

From Pythagoras to the Blues

One of humankind's earliest musical instruments was the hunting bow. Some ancestral huntsman or huntswoman realized one day that the "plunk" sound of the bowstring changed when the bow string was stretched more tightly or loosely. Many aboriginal peoples still use the bow to make music today. They simply place one end of the bow on the ground, and lean on the top end of the bow to stretch or loosen the bowstring as they pluck it. The effect is somewhat like a one-stringed bass fiddle, or "washtub bass".

2500 years ago the Greek metaphysician Pythagoras turned his brilliant mind to the question of why the bow string produced different sounds when stretched more or stretched less. He then discovered that lengths of string stretched between two points with equal tension would produce varying sounds depending on the length of the string.

Pythagoras began to experiment with the sounds produced by plucking different lengths of string. He soon noticed that if he plucked two strings simultaneously when one was exactly twice as long as the other, they would both produce sounds that somehow seemed very similar, even though the shorter string made a sound that was clearly higher.

We *now* know that the "half-as-long" string was vibrating exactly twice as fast as the longer string, and thus the shorter string was producing a second octave note which sounded very much like the longer string's first octave note. But the vibrational nature of sound was not discovered until nearly 1700 A.D., so Pythagoras could only compare the lengths of the strings with his feelings about the sounds that they produced.

Pythagoras plucked, and listened, some more. He reasoned that if the mathematical "ratio" of 2 to 1 (one string twice as long as the other) would produce two sounds that seemed so similar, perhaps other simple ratios like 3 to 2 or 4 to 3 could be applied to the lengths of vibrating strings to produce more sounds that somehow "related well" to each other.

So he continued his experimentation. He stretched a convenient length of string out, and plucked it to produce his first octave note. He then plunked his finger down exactly in the middle of the string, which created two lengths of string, each exactly one-half as long as the original. Each of these new "half-length" strings produced a second octave note when plucked. He then used a variety of simple mathematical ratios (like 5 to 4, 3 to 2, 4 to 3, etc.) to decide how he wanted to divide up these second octave lengths of string.

Eventually Pythagoras ended up by dividing each length of string into 12 equal sections. Why did he do it just this way? No one today knows for sure, but a quick look at a modern piano will clearly show that Pythagoras' 12 note octave division, known as the "**Chromatic Scale**", has stood the test of time!

Pythagoras' Chromatic Scale

We call this process of breaking up the octave distance into a number of smaller pieces "creating a scale". The word **scale** refers to some particular way of dividing that octave distance into pieces. Pythagoras' 12 note division (actually a 13 note division if you count the first and last note of the scale which are really the "same" notes, one octave apart) is called the **Chromatic Scale**. It is still the basic scale used by most of our Western civilization's music and musical instruments.

Look at the 12 note Chromatic scales built into the piano. A piano contains 6 or 8 Chromatic scales placed next to each other. As I mentioned, by the late middle ages each piano note had been assigned a letter name. Each white note is indicated by a simple letter name (C - D - E - F - G - A - B - C), but each black note has two names. For instance the black note between the white notes C and D, can be called *either* C# (C-sharp, meaning higher than C) or Db (D-flat, meaning lower than D). Same exact note, two names, just like a partially filled glass of water that can be called either "half-full" or "half-empty".

Read off each letter name on the piano, from any C note to the next highest C note. Notice that in one octave

I've used the b (flat) names for each black note, and in the next octave I've used all # (sharp) names. Right now, it's convenient for us to read the Chromatic scale to run from C to C, although it would be perfectly correct to read or play a Chromatic scale from an Eb to the next Eb, or from an A# to the next A#, or any other possible combination, as long as it began and ended with the same note. **Scales always begin and end on the same note, one Octave apart!**

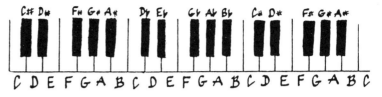

Major, Minor, & Blues Scales

In a way, we might consider a scale to be a kind of **"musical alphabet"**. By using the 26 letters of the English alphabet in various combinations we create English words, sentences, and literature. Using the letters of the Russian alphabet we create Russian words, sentences, and long dreary novels.

Just as many cultures have their own alphabet, most of the world's cultures have their own unique way of dividing up the octave distance. Thus each culture has a scale or scales that best suit its own musical tastes and traditions.

The notes of any particular culture's scale, be it a Gypsy scale, a Chinese scale, or a British scale, can be put together in various combinations to create music with a sound characteristic of that culture. Chinese music, for instance, sounds familiar and natural to the Chinese but may sound strange to American ears because it is based on a very different way of dividing the octave distance (that is, on a very different **scale**), than we are used to.

Pythagoras' 12 note scale was almost never used in its entirety. Instead, a certain number of notes were chosen from it (usually 7) to form what we might consider as "child" scales from their 12 note "mother". Each of these child scales had a particular sound or feel of its own. We could consider these child scales as dialects which come from a mother tongue, just as the Southern drawl, Yankee twang, and Cockney dialects are delightfully different ways of speaking "mother" English.

By the late middle ages, two of these child scales had become far more popular than any of the others that had been tried. These two most popular scales were named the **Major scale** and the **Minor scale**. Each has 7 notes. Each, like every scale, begins on a lower octave note and ends on the next higher octave note. But the way in which each scale's octave distance is divided up is different, and so each scale uses different notes. Thus music based on the Major Scale sounds quite dissimilar to the music of the Minor Scale.

The Major Scale eventually became the basis for much of Western Europe's music. It has a grand, strong, brassy feel, and was especially used for orchestral or marching music. The Major Scale tended to be used in the music of kings, and courts, and the upper classes.

The Minor Scale has a more plaintive or wistful quality. It was perhaps more popularly used in Eastern Europe than Western Europe, but more importantly, it tended to be the common folk's music. Gypsies, Jews, and Irish people, shepherds and sailors loved the brave mournful sound of the Minor Scale...

By the late 1950's, another "child" scale from Pythagoras' 12 note "mother" had taken the entire world by storm. This was the Blues Scale, born in America when the African musical traditions of the slave population merged with the Major and Minor scale traditions of their European captors. The Blues Scale is the basic "alphabet" from which most Blues, Rock, and Jazz music is created. It's probably the most popular scale that the planet has ever heard!

Here is a chart that compares all four scales that I've discussed so far. I have only used "flat names" (b) to represent the notes that are played by the black keys of the piano.

"C" Chromatic Scale :	C	Db	D	Eb	E	F	Gb	G	Ab	A	Bb	B	C	(13 notes from "C" to "C")
"C" Major Scale :	C		D		E	F		G		A		B	C	(8 notes from "C" to "C")
"C" Minor Scale :	C		D	Eb		F		G	Ab		Bb		C	(8 notes from "C" to "C")
"C" Blues Scale :	C			Eb		F	Gb	G			Bb		C	(7 notes from "C" to "C")

Appendix C: Zen and the Art of Blues Harp Blowing

Perhaps it does seem like a strange title – but it's not a joke. Because the psychological principles that underlie Zen and similar disciplines have recently been used to teach subjects as diverse as sports and drawing. Millions of people have learned new skills from books like *"Inner Tennis"*, *"Inner Skiing"* and *"Drawing on the Right Side of the Brain"*. And this same type of approach is exceptionally well-suited for the teaching of spontaneous, improvisational music such as blues harmonica!

The serious practitioners of Zen, Karate, Aikido, and Yoga often seem to possess nearly superhuman abilities. The best Zen archers can send an arrow straight to the target while blindfolded, the Karate and Aikido Masters can disarm a dozen simultaneous attackers, and the top-of-the-line Yogis can voluntarily suspend pulse and respiration. The adept students of more "Western" disciplines like self-hypnosis and "superlearning" often perform the slightly less herculean tasks of quitting smoking or learning 1500 words of a foreign language in a single day. What have these strange but impressive feats to do with would-be harmonica players?

As I've said elsewhere, there are two main ways of playing music. One way is to use a notation system (such as the simple one I've developed for harmonica) which tells us exactly what note to play, and when. I call this mode of playing "classical" music. We are repeating note for note a piece of music which someone considered enough of a classic to write down.

The other way is to learn the wonderfully exciting way of making music known as "improvising". This involves creating the music second by second as we are playing it. Improvising, or "jamming", is often done against a blues background provided by other musicians, although we can learn to do it alone as well.

When improvising, certain rules must be followed, but within these generalized rules the choice of notes is left to the player. Jamming can be one of the most freeing and self-expressive activities that you'll ever do in your life!

A Martial Arts Analogy

The student of Karate engages in two very different main types of training. On the technical level, he or she practices specific punches, kicks and blocks until they feel comfortable, natural and familiar. He or she will also practice a mental state known as **"one-pointedness"**. In this state the student is relaxed but totally focused on the attacker, so that whichever offensive or defensive move is needed will flow naturally without mental analysis or self-criticism.

Clearly, to criticize or analyze oneself in the midst of battle ("I should have kicked his kneecap, and then...") would distract concentration from the crucial present situation. Zen and the other disciplines mentioned above also use approximately the same "two-way" teachings to achieve their results (although the words used to label such teachings differ widely).

Improvisation: Locating the Mind's Ear

Learning the ability to improvise music requires similar preparation. We must practice certain technical skills, rules, and guidelines, starting with a few very simple instructions and building up to the more technically demanding ones. At the same time (if we want to improvise rather than play classical music) we'll have to begin to locate that mental state which blues and jazz musicians refer to as **"playing from the gut"** or **"playing with soul"**.

It's hard to describe that mental place in words. Some would say it's like being on "automatic pilot" after you've learned to drive well. Others might say it's like the state you're in when you've danced so freely and wildly (perhaps after drinking a few beers) that for just a few minutes you forgot to notice whether you were embarrassing your partner or not!

Perhaps it's even related to the way we can often begin a sentence without thinking and the words just flow out, unplanned yet mostly making sense. But regardless of how we might verbalize it, the following relaxation and visualization exercises will help you to get to that mental "place" most conducive to creating music!

I've built certain "high-tech" psychological teaching devices right into my package. Many of the recorded sections have "subliminal suggestions" (very softly recorded verbal instructions) to help you relax and not be critical of yourself while playing.

But your most important task is to allow yourself a few hours of freedom from self-criticism as you explore my book and cassette. Focus and concentrate on my written words, my voice, and the music. Don't permit those nagging, self-hating inner messages ("You can't do this you're tone-deaf" or "You didn't understand that part right away? You must be dumb") to distract you. Give 'em the day off! Most of my instructions are quite simple, and easily understood if you read or listen to them as many times as you need to, without "self-sabotage"!

Even if you are a hard-headed, skeptical, non-believer in "mystical" pursuits, these teaching techniques will work *for* you... whether you believe in them or not.

Visualization, Relaxation and Playing from the Gut

For many of us, it's difficult to create music spontaneously, without conscious thought. Especially if we have doubts about our musical abilities, free improvisation may seem like a hopelessly optimistic goal. Yet I believe that we all possess an internal reservoir of talent, if we can only learn to tap its hidden depth.

As I've already expressed in my section on "Zen and the Art of Blues Harp Blowing", improvised music flows from a very special place. A psycho-physiologist would probably prefer to label this place as the **right hemisphere** of the brain. A martial artist would call it **hara** or **one-point**, and a hypnotist the **self-induced trance**. The Zen monk might know such a space as **mushin** or **no-mind**, while the Southern Blues musician would advise you to **play from your gut**!

However, you choose to label this point from which improvised music flows most freely this exercise will help you to locate it.

The Exercise

Sit comfortably in a warm, quiet room. Make sure that your harmonica and tape deck are within easy reach, and that your tape casette is positioned to any of the backing music sections at the end of side two.

Tighten the muscles of your feet and hold them tensely for a second or two. Relax them. Do this once more. Travel upward through your body, tensing and relaxing, tensing and relaxing each muscle group. Calves, thighs, behind, stomach, chest, shoulders, arms, hands, neck, jaw and eyes. Then relax your entire body as completely as you can. Concentrate on feeling **warm and heavy, warm and heavy**. Say **"warm and heavy"** to yourself as you relax after tensing.

Now picture your body becoming filled up with a clear, luminous light or fluid. Let it flow through your feet, then up into your legs and trunk and head until it suffuses your entire being. Take as long as you like to picture this happening, **but try to visualize it as realistically as possible.**

If your mind tends to wander (it may at first, especially if you are unaccustomed to such exercises), return your attention to the inflowing luminous fluid as quickly and completely as you can, as soon as you notice that you've wandered. But please don't criticize yourself for wandering off.

The deeper your relaxation, and the clearer your image or visualization of the luminous fluid the more effective this type of technique (used by many Olympic athletes) can be. Many people find that listening to a section of backing music (and the accompanying subliminal suggestions) during the relaxation and visualization process helps to achieve a stronger effect with less effort. The only drawback to doing so is that you will have to rewind the tape before proceeding with the rest of the exercise.

Now that you're completely relaxed and "luminescent", you can use this altered state of consciousness in two ways.

A. Turn on one of my sections of backing music and just **visualize** the luminous fluid flowing out of you, through your harp, and producing beautiful, exciting Blues music along with the backing music. Or:

B. Turn on one of my sections of backing music and put your harp to your mouth (using slow, dreamy movements that don't reduce your relaxation). Picture the luminous fluid flowing out through your harp as you play anything that you like.

Try not to think at all about what you're playing. But if you must do something planned, use simple and general rules like the "Simple Jamm Rules" (page 41) or the "In and Out Twelve Bar" (page 42). Think as little as possible once you've decided upon the general rule that you'll be using to improvise with.

The more familiar and comfortable you are with the basic techniques and styles of playing that I've included in my instructions, the more options you will have at your disposal when you put your brain on "automatic pilot" and play from your gut!

You'll find that when you're ready to return to the so-called "real world", just take a few deep harmonica-player's breaths, stretch, and rise up feeling rested, energetic, and musical! And if you enjoy this way of looking at the world, please read the information on my newest book, *The Three Minute Meditator*.

Appendix D: More About Your Harmonicas

What's Wrong With My Harmonica?

So you just can't get a good sound out of certain holes on your harmonica. The sad truth is, from my fifteen years of harmonica teaching, that the fault, dear student, lies in your mouth.

I'd say, in general, that the chances are 95 out of 100 that the "problem" is not in the harmonica. I would raise those odds to 98 out of 100 if your problem is with the high notes (see page 29 for help), and to **99+ out of 100** if your problem is with the number 2 In note (see page 32, and be patient).

Of course, you might say that if the 2 In always plays hard to get, then it *is* the harmonica's fault. Maybe so, but *all* the C harmonicas are like that, and returning yours to the factory for replacement is like buying and eating bushels of red hot chili peppers, in the hopes of finding a sweet one...

Speaking of returning harmonicas (in case you sincerely believe that something is wrong with yours), here are the current addresses of the three main harmonica manufacturers. They will all repair or replace their products in the event of a factory defect. **Health regulations prevent us from testing harmonicas prior to sale, and from accepting returns, so please send your questions or the harmonica in question *directly* back to its manufacturer.**

Huang Harmonica: 12-A Seabro Avenue   North Amityville, NY 11701
Hohner Harmonica: P.O. Box 15035   Richmond, VA 23227
Lee Oskar Harmonica: P. O. Box 918   Cedar Glen, CA 92321

How Long Do Harmonicas Last?

All of the harmonicas recommended on page 6 are good ones. But even good harmonicas don't last long if they are not well cared for.

- If you don't follow the harmonica care instructions on page 6, your axe may only last for a few weeks.
- If you generally follow them, your instrument may well last for a few months.
- If you follow them *very* carefully, it should stay in good shape for many months or even years.
- In Volume II, my section on "Open Harp Surgery" will allow you to tune and repair your own harmonica.

Reach Out and Harp Somebody...

As of Fall 1993, I am in the process of setting up a non-profit corporation to help bring the joys of harmonica to some of the groups that I most like to work with: Adults and children with disabilities, people in nursing homes, people who are blind, and the terminally ill. Why do this? Because playing harp increases self-esteem and lung capacity, and reduces stress. Plus, doing it makes makes *Me* feel good!

Think it might make *You* feel good to help me in this work? You can make a donation (tax deductible, as soon as we finish setting up the organization). Or you can identify a group that needs music (nursing home, shelter, hospital, etc.), and we'll help you to work with them! Sound good, do good, feel good!

Moneyback Guarantee

• If your book or tape cassette arrives in a defective condition please write or call us so that we can replace it free of charge.

• If your harmonica arrives in defective condition please see page 58. Addresses of the manufacturers are included. They will repair or replace factory defective items.

• If you make a sincere effort to use this instructional package and feel that it has not worked for you, we will promptly refund the purchase price of the book and tape, if returned to us in undamaged condition.

Some Respect and Support

Although I enjoy and respect the contributions of the many excellent young American and British Blues and Rock bands, I feel that in these days of publicity hype and media overkill it is easy to overlook the original people and culture that gave us the Blues music. I've been blessed with the ability to convey information clearly, but I'm also very aware that my contribution rests entirely upon the shoulders of the Bluesmen and Blueswomen that came before. So if any of those original Bluespeople come your way – catch their shows, buy their records, go up to them after a show and shake their hands – they've given us more than we can repay.

Mr. J.C. Burris (left) and his uncle, Sonny Terry. (R.I.P.)

The Scale of the Universe

Many people consider music to be just a pleasant diversion or at most a popular art form, but fortunately Pythagoras was not one of these narrow minded folk. For the form and structure of music appear to be reflections of the entire universe, from atom to galaxy.

The Greeks used ratio theory (the science of the mathematical relationships of one thing to another) with great success in many different disciplines. Ratios determined the idealized physical proportions of the human body, so that the length of a statue's head had a particular mathematical ratio relative to the length of the body, and the girth of the arms bore a specific relationship to that of the legs. But Pythagoras was not merely grinding his favorite theoretical axe when he applied mathematical ratios to the distances between notes. I say this because the musical notes that he obtained and the ratios that he used to produce them have a far, far wider application than he knew (or did he?). Strangely enough, even though other cultures have scales of vastly varying size and complexity (the Chinese scale has 5 notes and the East Indian 22), many of the notes used in **all** cultures are the same. It's possible that this amazingly widespread usage of certain notes is due "only" to the psychological and physical properties that all human beings have in common. But this explanation, based as it is on the **human** experience, cannot begin to explain why Pythagoras' ratio itself (not just the notes) appears to possess an awesome universality. For it seems that both the ratio of the distances between the sun and the planets of the solar system, and the ratio of the distances between the quantum levels of energy in the molecule bear a strong similarity to–you guessed it–the ratios used by Pythagoras in determining scale structure.

Perhaps we human beings are just unlucky enough to be **the wrong size** to appreciate the flabbergastingly high degree of unity in all creation. But although I can scarcely keep my desk top in order, I am proud to be even a small, disorganized part of what I consider to be "God's Mind".

L. DA VINCI

If you look deeply enough into anything, you can learn something about everything.